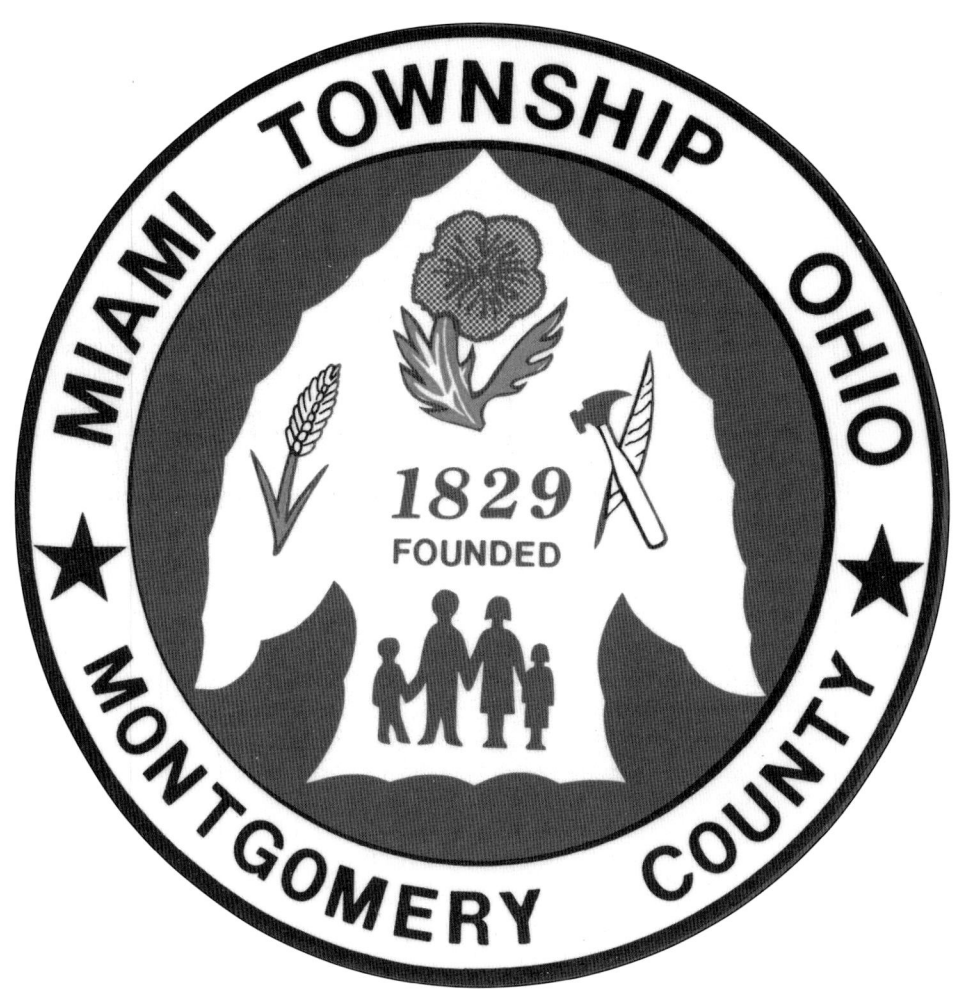

Created by Trustee Berman Layer in the early 1980s, the Miami Township logo features the date (1829) the township was founded. The arrowhead represents the Miami tribe of Native Americans who once inhabited the area. The flower is the Miami mistflower (so called by the Miami Indians), which was indigenous to the region at that time. The quill crossed with a hammer represents commerce and industry, and the family of four, the people who live and work in the township. The background is blue, representing the flowing Miami River, the earliest form of transportation. The circle represents unity with the State of Ohio's circular seal.

This book is dedicated, with thanks, to all those who came to Miami Township before us, to those whose commitment and service today make this an ideal place to live and work, and to future generations in the hope they will continue our efforts to balance suburban living with the preservation of green space and of the river that gave Miami Township its name.

175th Anniversary Committee

Copyright © 2004 by 175th Anniversary Committee
ISBN 0-7385-3328-9

Published by Arcadia Publishing
Charleston SC, Chicago IL, Portsmouth NH, San Francisco CA

Printed in Great Britain

Library of Congress Catalog Card Number: 2004108464

For all general information contact Arcadia Publishing at:
Telephone 843-853-2070
Fax 843-853-0044
E-mail sales@arcadiapublishing.com
For customer service and orders:
Toll-Free 1-888-313-2665

Visit us on the internet at http://www.arcadiapublishing.com

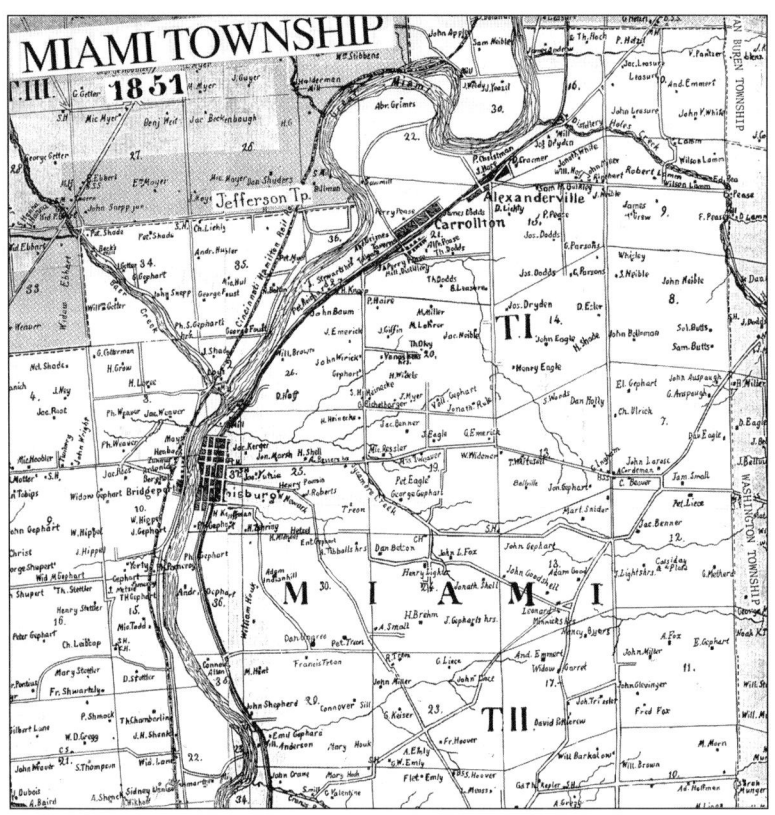

When this map was drawn in 1851, the villages of Carrollton and Alexanderville, Bridgeport and Miamisburg were all part of Miami Township. The names of several landowners listed on the map are still familiar to 21st-century township residents: Gephart, Pease, Heincke, Benner, Dryden, Lamme, and Munger.

CONTENTS

Acknowledgments		6
Introduction		7
1.	Township Prehistory: Before 1829	9
2.	Organizing a Township: 1829–1899	17
3.	20th Century Progress: 1900–1959	27
4.	The "Urban" Township: 1960–1980	41
5.	From Footpaths to Airports: 1797–1960	55
6.	Tobacco, Paper, and Nuclear Energy: 1800s–1992	67
7.	The Miami Valley Chautauqua: 1896–1946	79
8.	First Churches and Schools: 1803–1927	91
9.	Historic Events: 1800s–1988	107
10.	Township Government—Service First: 1829–2004	115
Further Reading		127

Acknowledgments

The efforts of many individuals and groups made this book possible: Jim Foster, Julia Hagwood, Lee Hieronymus, Shirley Omietanski, Jane Wildermuth, and Linda Zimmer outlined the book, did research, located photographs, and chose the images for these pages. Supporting the History Committee's efforts were the other members of Miami Township's 175th Anniversary Committee: Cindy Coffey, John DiPietro, Linda Galaise, Greg Hanahan, Charles Lewis, Judy Osborne, Sue Peterson, Jay Phares, Deborah Preston, and Annamarie Smith.

The local community was also involved. Trudi Callahan recommended our project to Harriet Foley, of the Franklin Historical Society, who loaned us Chautauqua information and photographs—including pictures from the museum's walls. So did Farmers and Merchants Bank in Miamisburg and Mike Minns at the Dayton Mall.

Laura Bornhorst, Nita Petticrew, Bobbye Sweny, and Les Wead of the Miamisburg Historical Society worked with us, as did the West Carrollton Historical Society, and the Miami Township, Miamisburg, and West Carrollton branch libraries. Additional photographs came from local churches, the Miamisburg Board of Education (and Ruth Yung, secretary to the superintendent of schools), and Wright State University's Special Collections and Archives.

Peggy Fox Geer, Donald Huber, Theresa and the late Charles Huber, Berman Layer, the Mote family, Tim Oren, Robert Siebenthaler, Sue and Bruce Walker, Jim and Diane Woolf, and *Miamisburg/West Carrollton News* editor Steve Sandlin loaned us irreplaceable photographs. They, along with Shirley Scarborough and Verda Seiber at Zion Evangelical Lutheran Church and the Reverend Ray Kiser at Zion United Church of Christ, also provided information about the pictures' history. Mark Renwick and Dave Neuhardt of the Miami and Erie Canal Society reviewed their postcard collections for images that Mark scanned for us.

Research material was provided by the Brane family, EvaMay Cox at St. John's Lutheran Church, former township trustee Byron (Barney) Grooms, Nikki Bailey Marshall, Andrew Sawyer of Sunwatch, Frank Schacherer, Ron Wilson (Miami Township school information), the Miamisburg School District, and the Ohio Historical Society.

Huston Beals, Elmer Gaffney, Harriet Hieronymus, and Esther Light have passed away, but left behind photographs that keep them, and yesterday's Miami Township, alive in memory. Pictures of the township today were provided by Kenneth Hagwood and Paul Tucker, along with members of the Fire, Police, Service, and Planning and Zoning Departments, and the Park Board. Jay Vada's scans made faded photographs come alive. Additional scanning was done by Stephen Hagwood and by Toni Jeske at Wright State University.

Our editor at Arcadia, Melissa Basilone, could not have been more helpful. With her support, the 175th Anniversary Committee has been able to meet the stringent deadline schedule we set for Arcadia: from first query to completed book in about eight months.

Thank you all for making this book possible—and thanks, too, to those who read it. We wrote it so you can see what Miami Township once was, as well as what it is today.

—Beth Tucker, project coordinator

Introduction

"When signal fires were lighted by the Mound Builders of old,
When Indians followed forest trails through winter's ice and cold,
Ere Columbus sailed with courage across an unknown sea,
Or the lowly Nazarene wandered beside fair Galilee;
Then, as now, thou were flowing forever and forever
Through ages of silence, O beautiful river.

"Today, bearing with thee the tide of the years,
Our joys and our sorrows, our hopes and our fears,
Flow on at low stage, or the flood's rapid motion.
Like thee, we move on to eternity's ocean,
Till rest shall be found in the peace of the Giver,
Onward, flow onward, O beautiful river."

"The Great Miami River"
—Seymour Tibbals

The history of Miami Township begins with the prehistoric Mound Builders, followed by later Native Americans including the Miami. In his poem, "The Great Miami River," Seymour Tibbals tells of the river that flows onward—and also of those it flows past.

More than 200 years ago, in October 1788, the "beautiful river" brought Judge John Cleves Symmes and an exploration party to the corner of southwestern Ohio, located between the Great Miami and Little Miami Rivers. Seven years later, D.C. Cooper cut a road along the east side of the Great Miami River, then east to today's Mad River Road, then north to Dayton.

About this time, the first European settlers arrived, traveling the rough footpaths bordering the river. Their early settlements were named Bridgeport and Miamisburg (which make up today's Miamisburg), Alexanderville, and Carrollton (today's West Carrollton). All were located in what would become Miami Township, established on December 9, 1829.

Over the years, the river and the township have seen many changes. Native Americans and wild game no longer roam the dense forests. The Mad River Trail and the first rough paths along the Great Miami's banks have been replaced by miles of paved roadways that crisscross the township. Many of the locks along the once bustling Miami and Erie Canal have disappeared, along with the tobacco barns and warehouses, the gristmills and paper mills built along the river's banks.

For centuries, the river has brought people and progress to the area—and it has also brought spring floods that have destroyed what had been built. But the river remains, as do photographs capturing memories of earlier times.

In these images, garnered from local historical societies, libraries, and longtime residents, Miami Township's earliest families, businesses, and buildings live on, along with the Miami Valley Chautauqua, the canal, and the area between Miamisburg and West Carrollton called "the Narrows," where five forms of transportation once ran side by side.

Early residents of Miami Township included the Fox family, who farmed acreage on Swamp Road (today's Spring Valley Road). Like many other landowners in the late 19th and early 20th centuries, Tom and Ohmer Fox occasionally made time to take a buggy ride. (Courtesy of Peggy Fox Geer.)

One
TOWNSHIP PREHISTORY
Before 1829

Evidence of the existence of prehistoric man in Ohio is abundant. Earthworks built by the early Mound Builders have been found in many parts of the state, but the Miamisburg Mound, at 68 feet in height and 800 feet in circumference, is the largest conical mound.

Later Native Americans, including the Shawanoes (Shawnee) and the Miamis who hunted, fished, and farmed in the area, had no knowledge of the Mound Builders or their culture. Between the 1600s and the mid-1700s, the Miamis had occupied the southwestern part of the state, and roving bands of Shawanoes ranged north of the Ohio River.

But four of the American colonies, Virginia, New York, Connecticut, and Massachusetts, also claimed portions of the territory northwest of the Ohio River based on charters granted by the kings of England. In 1784, the first Congressional Committee was appointed to prepare a plan for the disposal of these western lands.

The committee was faced with several problems: Revolutionary War veterans were demanding the land bounties that had been promised them; squatters were crossing the Ohio River and staking claims; there was a need for revenue to pay the national debt (Congress did not have the power to tax at that time); and procedures for the survey and sale of the western lands were needed. The Land Ordinance of May 20, 1785, resolved these issues.

Three years later, Judge John Cleves Symmes came with an exploration party to the land that would become Miami Township. His record, dated October 12, 1788, reads: "on the 22nd ult., I landed at Miami and explored the country as high as the upper side of the fifth range of townships." This range line cuts through the southern part of the corporate limits of today's Miamisburg.

After D.C. Cooper cut a road through the territory in 1795, the first settlers arrived. Symmes sold land and later forfeited it to the government because of his failure to pay. Those who had purchased land from him were given special preemption privileges by an act of Congress in 1799.

James Byers was one of those who took advantage of this act. He purchased Section 17 in Township II, Range 5, three miles southeast of Miamisburg, on September 1, 1799. Others took advantage of privileges granted by Congress in 1800. Dr. John Hole purchased the north half of Section 25 and the north half of Section 31 on December 25, 1801. Zachariah Hole purchased the south half of these two sections. Together, these sections include almost all of the territory now occupied by the city of Miamisburg.

Other pioneers included George Adams of Revolutionary War fame, who bought sections in Carrollton; Anthony Chevalier, a Revolutionary War soldier; Col. William Dodds; James Drew; and David Lamme. To the west of the river came Alexander Scott, William Emrick, G. Myers, P. Gebhart, George Stettler, and Samuel Tibbals.

Industry began in 1802 when William Lamme and his family came from Kentucky and established the first gristmill in a gorge between the hills of Hole's Creek in the northeast corner of the township.

Early residents' access to religion and medicine also predated the formation of the township. Stettler and St. John's (Gebhart) churches were formed, and John Jacob LaRose, a minister of the German Reformed church, purchased 160 acres one mile southeast of Hole's Station. Two doctors, John and Peter Treon, arrived at Hole's Station in 1811.

Ohio's Mound Builders included several early groups or "cultures," each named for the persons on whose land the mounds were discovered or for the places where the mounds were found. Although the state's largest conical mound is the Miamisburg Mound, smaller mounds were once located in the area that became Carrollton and Alexanderville. No trace of the smaller mounds remains today.

Esther Light, whose essays were published in *Miamisburg: The Story of Our Town*, told this story: the Miamisburg area "lay almost wholly within a circular earthwork created by the Mound Builders. Early settlers estimated that the earthwork's walls stood from three to ten feet in height, and were fifty feet wide at the base. Huge trees grew on the walls, and brick made of its clay went into the houses of the town."

About the Miamisburg Mound, she wrote: "History relates that the Mound was built by the Adena Indians, who occupied most of the Miami Valley from 1,000 B.C. to 500 A.D. The Mound which they built here is the largest of its kind in the Eastern United States. It stands on a 100-foot bluff south of the town (and) the base occupies about one and a half acres. Consider the herculean task of building such a structure in the days when a wheelbarrow was unknown, when man had only his own skills and primitive tools."

She added: "The purpose of the Mound has never been clearly defined. It has been classified as burial, signal or sacrificial—perhaps all three. Although there are disputes, the majority of historians consider it to be a burial mound.

"In 1839, a man by the name of Lewis obtained permission to dig for water at the Mound site. In his digging, he found some bones which were later carefully preserved by the owner of the Mound and the surrounding acreage, Dr. John Treon.

"Later, in 1869, a group of citizens attempted to ascertain the purpose of the Mound by sinking a shaft from the top. About eight feet below the summit, a human skeleton in a sitting position was discovered. At 24 feet, a number of flat stones, suggesting an altar set on an angle of 45 degrees, were found. The project, however, was abandoned before the base was reached.

"The Mound and the surrounding area became a park when Charles Kettering bought it in 1920 from the heirs of Dr. John Treon. Kettering gave the land, with historical site, to the state of Ohio." (Courtesy of the Miamisburg Historical Society, Alfred Cade photograph.)

The recorded history of Native Americans in the Ohio Valley may begin around 1667, when La Salle discovered and descended the Ohio River. In 1682, he referred to the Shawanoes "from the valley of the Ohio, whose following embraced 150 warriors (who) came to ask the protection of the French against the all-destroying Iroquois." By 1740, the Miamis inhabited the western part of Ohio; bands of Shawanoes ranged north of the Ohio River. (Map from *The Indian Tribes of Ohio*.)

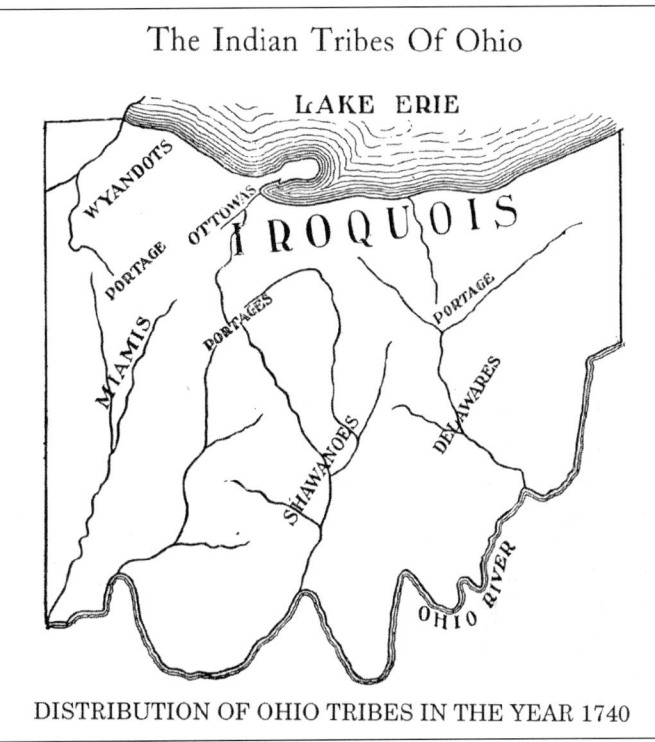

What remains as evidence of Ohio's once powerful tribes of Miami, Shawanoe (Shawnee), Iroquois, Delaware, Ottawa, and Wyandot? Nothing but a few graves and village sites here and there, or scattered monuments. In the names of the state's rivers, creeks, and townships, early settlers preserved the fact that Native Americans once lived in Ohio—including Miami Township along the Miami River. (Courtesy of the Miamisburg Historical Society.)

PETITION TO CONGRESS BY CITIZENS OF HAMILTON COUNTY

[LC:HF:6 Cong., 1 sess.:DS]

[July 13, 1799]

The Territorial Papers of the United States
Compiled and edited by
Clarence Edwin Carter
Volume III
The Territory Northwest of the River Ohio, 1787-1803
Continued
United States Government Printing Office
Washington: 1934

To the Senate and house of Representatives of the United States

The Memorial of the Subscribers, Citizens of the County of Hamilton in the Territory of the United States, North West of River Ohio, humbly sheweth, that your Memorialists, knowing that Judge Symmes had contracted with the board of Treasury of the United States for a large Tract of land, lying between the great and little Miami Rivers, and believing that, that Contract would be carried into effect, not knowing the circumstances under which it stood, have at different times become purchasers under him, and have at a very considerable expence and with much difficulty, left their former habitations and moved on the Lands which they had thus purchased.

Your Memorialists are and always have been ignorant of the facts by which Judge Symmes has forfieted his claim, ___ they saw the Contract with the board of Treasury accompanied with the Opinion of the Attorney General of the United States, published in the public prints, and it was under the sanction of that Opinion that most of your Memorialists innocently became purchasers.

Your Memorialists have seen a Law passed at the last Session of Congress making Provision for disposing of the Lands in question, and it with Pleasure they Percieve that your honorable Body has taken their unhappy Case into consideration, as it is a conclusive Proof that the United States are disposed to treat them with tenderness, but they also Percieve with Pain and regret that the Provisions of the Bill are by no means sufficient to afford the intended Relief.

Many of your Memorialists have Purchased since the Month of April 1797 and some of them since the commencement of the present year of Persons to whom Judge Symmes had sold a right of Preemption and are therefore wholly excluded from the Provisions of the Bill, some of them have settled on lots given by the supposed Proprietors to encourage and Promote the settleme[n]t of the Country, some of them have expended large sum[s] of money in erecting Mills and all of them have spent mu[ch] time and labour in opening roads and erecting temporary Bridges, some of your memorialists placed such imp[li]cit confidence in the integrety of Judge Symmes, that they neglected or thought it not necessary, to reduce their Contracts to writing—others relying on the same security (which unfortunately is like to fail them) have paid him considerable sums of Money, without ever taking a Receipt, and many have Purchased of Agents and of persons claiming under Judge Symmes without knowing the circimstances of the Preceeding conveyances.

Your Memorialists have paid their money to Judge Symmes under a belief that he had a right to receive it, it will therefore be impossible for them to advance the sum called for by Government until they recover it from his hands, this must necessarily require a con[si]derable time as he absolutely refuses to refund a Cen[t] under a pretence that he must hold it to defray the expence of his intended suit against the United [States].

The difficulty and the delay that will attend a Pr[ose]cution against the first Judge of the General Court [who] claims and enjoys the Priviledge of freedom from ar[rest] and bail are too evident not to be dreaded, it will [there]fore be absolutely impossible for your Memorialists [to] make the Payments as they are required by the Present law, which was not made known to them till it was too late to comply with its requisitions had they possessed the means, as the law was not Published in the Country till late in the Month of June. Unless therefore the Justice and humanity of Congres can devise for them a more effectual relief they have no Prospect, but that of distress and ruin. The great sacrifice made by those who retire from[m] a settled Country into the midst of a Wilderness exposed to the ravages of the Indians, the in[cle]mency of the Seasons and the want of the common necessaries of life can be known only to themselves —this sacrifice your Memorialists have made under a full conviction that they were laying a foundation for their future ease; many of them have numerous families of Children, which they have brought with them from comfortable dwellings and have expended all they Possessed in Purchasing and improving the land, which they fondly imagined became thereby their own, feeling themselves thus secure, they toiled with chearfulness, supposing they toiled for themselves and were not awakened to a sence of their danger, till it became too late to escape it.

Your Memorialists are sincerely dissirous of complying with the terms of Congress as far as their ability will admit, they re willing to Pay the Price of the land, if they can be indulged with time sufficient to enable them to Prepare for the Payments, it is impossible for them to say how soon this preparation can be made, as it will depend in most cases on the event of suits against Judge Symmes; they have reason to fear that two or three years may elapse, before the money can be recovered from his hands, and until this is done, but few of them can make the first Payment,—Should it be consistent with the views of Congress, to remove the forfieture contemplated in the present bill, in case of failure in any of the Payments at the Periods stipulated, and in stead thereof to Provide for Securing a title to the settlers, on their giving sufficient security to Pay the sums of money with lawful Interest from the days on which they became due, it would releive your Memorialists from the danger they apprehend of loosing large sums of money in attempting to save their lands by a compliance with the terms of Congress.

Your Memorialists pray that your Honorable Body will take the premises into consideration and grant such Relief as your humanity and Wisdom may dictate.–

Judge John Cleves Symmes and land speculators from New Jersey persuaded the Confederation Congress in 1787 to sell 1,000,000 acres of western lands lying north of the Ohio River between the two Miami rivers. Judge Symmes had become interested in this land through the recommendation of Benjamin Stites, a soldier and trader to whom Symmes granted land near the Little Miami.

Symmes never paid for nor developed the full 1,000,000 acres he sought. According to Dr. George Knepper (in *The Official Ohio Lands Book*), Symmes mishandled his land survey and sales to such an extent that Congress restricted his purchase to 311,682 acres, including lands reserved for special purposes.

On occasion, Symmes sold land lying outside the boundaries of his purchase. Sometimes his associates back in New Jersey inadvertently sold lots that Symmes had already sold to others—and the reverse was true as well.

Those who unwittingly purchased land that Symmes sold beyond the limits of his possession, and those who settled on that land, were technically squatters on federal land. To correct this situation, Congress passed relief acts in March 1799 and March 1801, which gave these settlers the first right to buy their land from the federal government. This was the first time the right of preemption was granted by Congress.

A number of Hamilton County (which predated Miami Township) settlers signed a July 1999 petition to Congress (pictured above), asking for assistance because they had already "paid their money to Judge Symmes under a belief that he had a right to receive it." Among them were James Byers; James Pettierew (Petticrew); John Vance; William, David and Nathan Lamme; George Adams; William Vanarsdol and frontiersman Seimon (Simon) Kenton; surveyor Daniel C. Cooper; and Dayton's first postmaster and school teacher, Benjamin Van Cleve. (Courtesy of the Miamisburg Historical Society.)

The Symmes Purchase began at the Ohio River and ran approximately 24 miles northward, between the Great Miami and Little Miami Rivers. Although Judge Symmes contracted for 1,000,000 acres, President Washington signed a deed in 1794 conveying to Symmes 248,250 acres plus a surveying township. Congress allowed one-third of a dollar off for "bad lands" and incidental charges, so Symmes actually paid two-thirds of a dollar per acre. (Map from *Ohio Lands: A Short History*.)

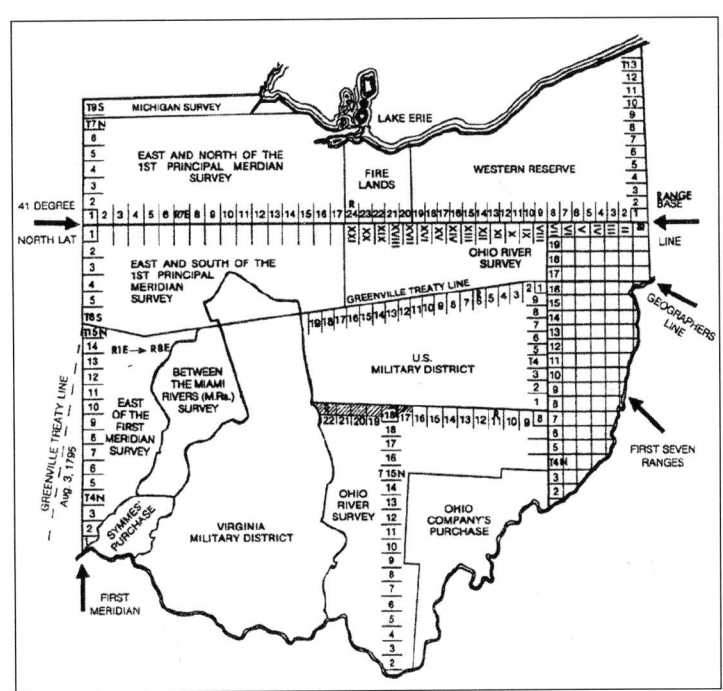

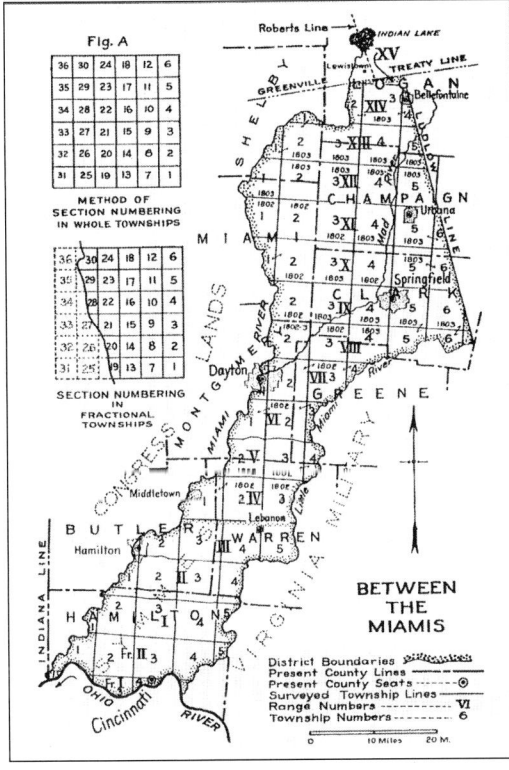

The Symmes Purchase was privately surveyed. It is the only original land survey in the U.S. that has ranges running south to north and fractional townships running west to east. Sections were numbered according to the Land Ordinance of 1785. The federal surveys (located above the Symmes Purchase) continued Symmes' unorthodox numbering of ranges and townships, so that the "Between the Miami Rivers" survey was consistent. (Map from *Ohio Lands: A Short History*.)

Daniel Gebhart's tavern at Old Main and Lock Streets was the first in the area. In 1805, Valentine Gebhart and his family, including sons Andrew, Philip, and Daniel, came to Hole's Station (today's Miamisburg). Daniel acquired land and laid out the second plat of the town in 1818, but he opened his tavern as early as 1811. Eventually the tavern became a boarding house, but today it has been restored to serve as a museum. (Courtesy of *The Miamisburg/West Carrollton News*.)

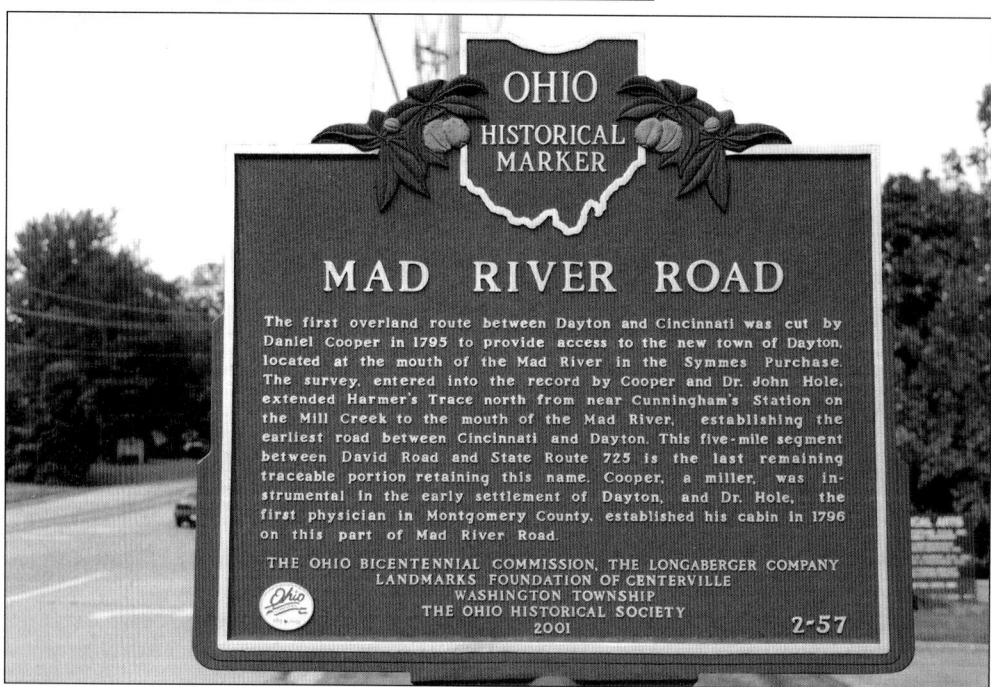

One of the earliest roads between Cincinnati and Dayton is commemorated on this historical marker near the corner of Mad River and Miamisburg-Centerville Roads. The marker describes a 1797 survey for Mad River Road recorded in the Hamilton County road book, citing "an order of Court to Daniel Cooper, Daniel Griffing and John Hole on a petition of more than 12 citizens" that a 38.75-mile road "was made and reported." (Courtesy of Paul Tucker.)

On February 20, 1818, four men from Pennsylvania, Emanuel Gebhart, Jacob Kercher, Dr. John Treon, and Dr. Peter Treon, his uncle, offered for sale "a large number of lots (90) in a new town by the name of Miamisburg. (I)t is divided into squares, each lot containing the fifth part of an acre, also public grounds gratis in the center." The first plat was bounded by Commercial, Race, Walnut, and Water Streets. (Courtesy of the Miamisburg Historical Society, R.L Penwell drawing.)

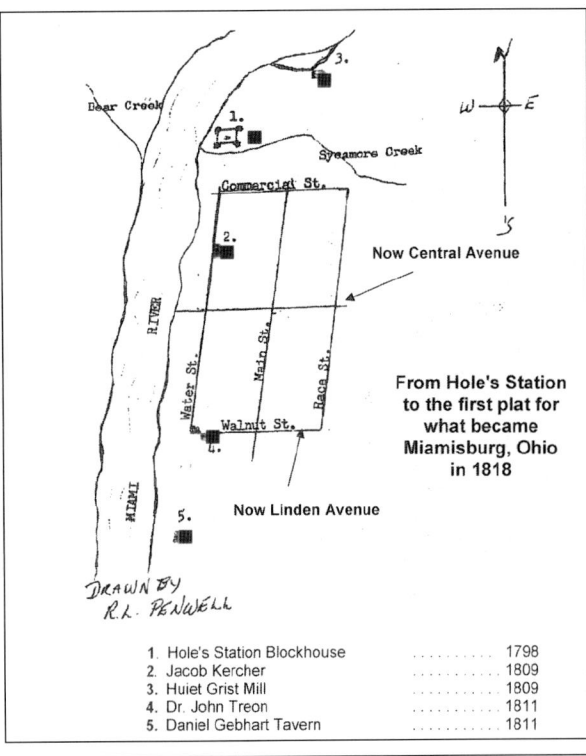

From Hole's Station to the first plat for what became Miamisburg, Ohio in 1818

1. Hole's Station Blockhouse 1798
2. Jacob Kercher 1809
3. Huiet Grist Mill 1809
4. Dr. John Treon 1811
5. Daniel Gebhart Tavern 1811

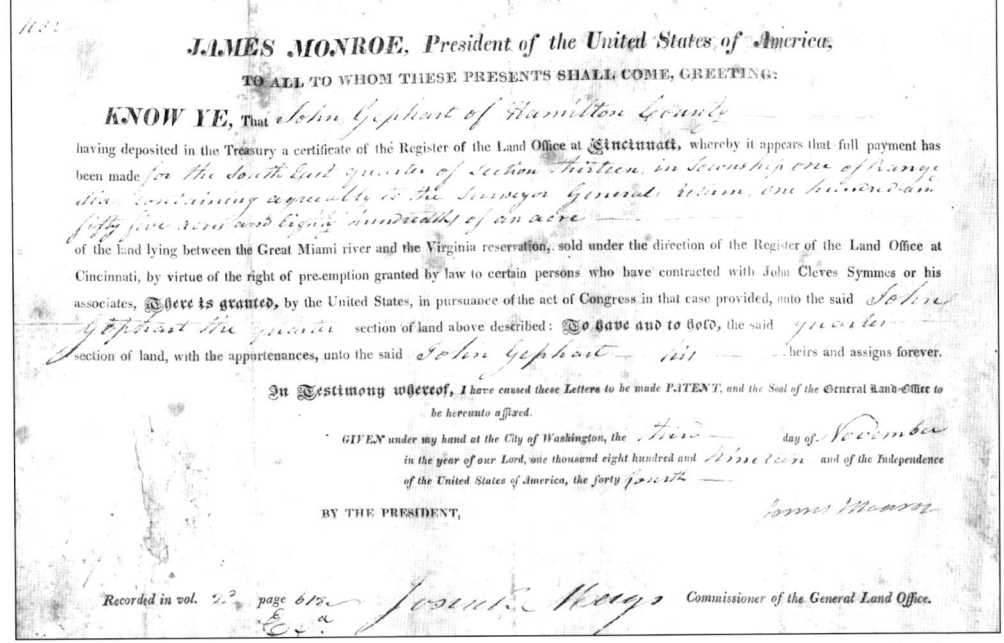

President James Monroe's name heads an 1819 deed that granted John Gephart and his heirs a quarter section of land in Hamilton County (Miami Township), Section 13, Township I, Range 5. Gephart, who had originally purchased the land (located between the Great Miami River and the Virginia Reservation) from Judge John Cleves Symmes and his associates, received the land by virtue of the right of preemption. (Courtesy of Lee Hieronymus.)

OHIO MAP IN 1803 WHEN THE STATE WAS ADMITTED TO THE UNION

On March 1, 1803, Ohio became the 17th state to enter the Union. Its entry was based on the Northwest Ordinance, the Enabling Act of 1802, and the Ohio constitution adopted in November 1802.

Formal Congressional admittance of Ohio into the Union, however, failed to take place until passage of a joint resolution of Congress on August 7, 1953 (to take effect as of March 1, 1803). This 150-year lapse in formal admittance did not affect Ohio's legal status as a state.

Ohio's first capitals were in the east at Chillicothe and at Zanesville before the state offices moved to Columbus. Centrally located, Columbus was still a wilderness when it was designated the permanent state capital in February 1812.

When Ohio became a state in 1803, Montgomery County (in which Miami Township is located) extended to the state's northern border. Those who purchased land from Judge Symmes lived in Hamilton County, which had been established in 1790, as Butler and Montgomery counties weren't formed until 1803. (Map from *Ohio Lands: A Short History*.)

Two
Organizing a Township
1829–1899

Miami Township was created by an act of the Montgomery County commissioners on December 9, 1829. Originally, it was part of Washington Township, but the commission decided that Washington Township was too large and split the territory.

In the beginning, all of the new township lay east of the Miami River. Additional land came from Van Buren Township. Additions from German Township, west of the river, were made in 1831 and 1841, until the area of the township was placed at 40 square miles.

The *Combination Atlas Map of Montgomery County, Ohio*, published in 1875, describes the township in these words: "This place was organized as a Township about the year 1830, and Emanuel Gebhart was the first Justice of the Peace….The soil is of a limestone nature, and very productive. At one time fruit in its wild nature grew spontaneously; and the early pioneers had easy access to plentiful supplies of wild plums, strawberries, and grapes. Wild bees were very plentiful. The streams that flow through this rich Township were literally dense with fish; and it was a common occurence, even for those least skilled with piscatorial knowledge, to capture with a seive enough fish to fill eight tubs at *one haul*. Deer, turkeys, wolves, and other game were abundant. Squirrels were so numerous that farmers were induced to offer a reward for every tail brought to them. This mode was adopted in order to effect [sic] a decrease in the ranks of the mischievous little animals, who played sad havoc with our old pioneer fathers' crops."

At Miami Township's first election, which took place at the Charles Connelly Tavern in Miamisburg on April 5, 1830, voters chose three trustees (John Neibel, Fletcher Emly, and Benjamin Sayre), a clerk (Thomas Morton), a treasurer (Charles Connelly), and a constable (Andrew Treon). Today's voters still elect three trustees and a clerk-treasurer, each to a four-year term of office.

When township residents voted for governor of the state of Ohio in 1830, there were 231 votes cast. From a handful of early settlers living in log cabins, the population had grown, and handsome frame and brick homes were under construction in Miamisburg, Carrollton, and Alexanderville (also known as Alexandersville).

Much of the history of Miami Township intertwines with that of these early towns and villages. They were one at the beginning, and later assumed separate and distinct identities, although the city of Miamisburg still lies within the township's boundaries.

From the late 1860s to 1969, township government was conducted in a gray brick building on Central Avenue in Miamisburg. It was sold at auction in 1969 and torn down in 1970 to make way for a drive-in facility for a bank. A new township building was constructed on Lyons Road near the central business district in 1970.

While change has come to most facets of township life in the past 175 years, township government has remained constant. The trustee system of government, the oldest form of continuous active government in the United States, was established in 1830 and remains today. To be sure, the township constable has been replaced by a police chief and a modern police force, and the township school board no longer exists. Nor is there a justice of the peace or a fence surveyor, but there is a zoning inspector who acts as a member of an efficient planning and zoning department.

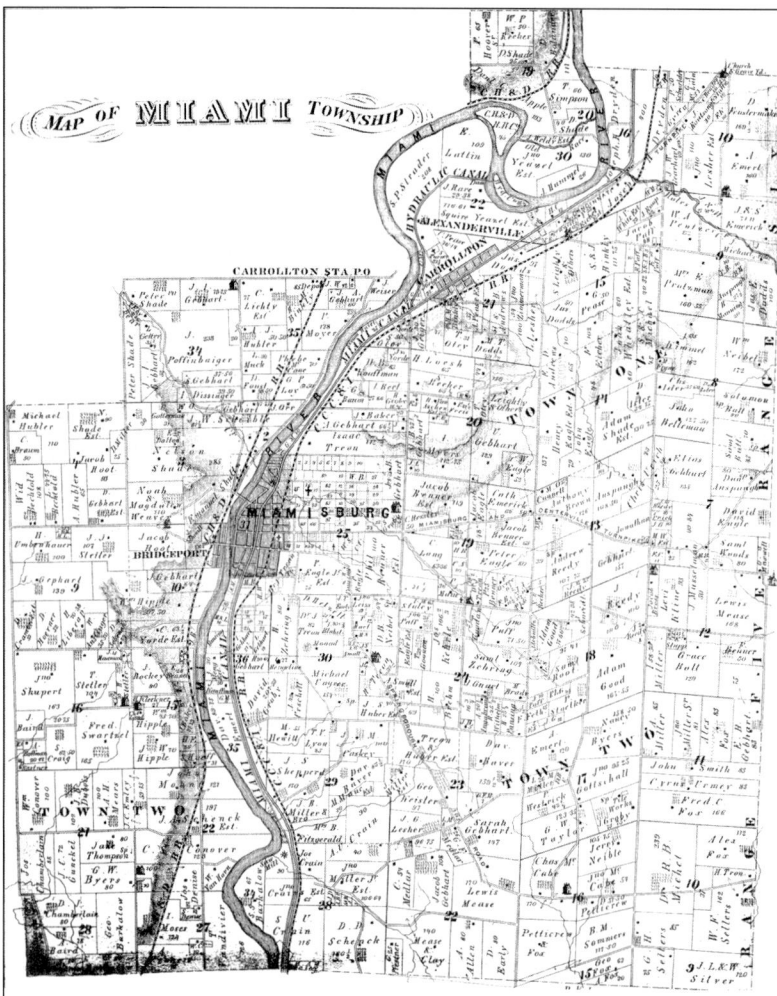

In 1875, when this map was drawn, Miami Township still included the communities of Carrollton and Alexanderville, Miamisburg, and Bridgeport. Little is known today about the towns of Bridgeport, once located at the west end of Miamisburg's Linden Avenue bridge, or Danville (near Alexanderville), except that Danville was famous for its boat-building business in the days of the Miami and Erie Canal, and Bridgeport was a small neighborhood that included only two streets, with a cooper shop, a row or two of houses, and the Railroad Saloon.

In the early days, when the township had been in existence for less than 50 years, the history of the area was summarized by the *Combination Atlas Map of Montgomery County*: "The first settlers of Miami (Township) came here about the year 1800. Among them were the Dodds, Lambs (Lammes), Adams, Vernosdells (Van Arsdales or Van Ausdalls) and Anthony Chevalier, the last-named being an old Revolutionary soldier. These individuals settled in the northern part of the township. A man by the name of Hole located the place, which was named after him, Hole's Station; it is now called Miamisburg. The first flouring-mill was erected in or about the year 1800, by Mr. Lamb, on Hole's Creek; and this Mr. Lamb also succeeded in building a house without the use of nails. The pristine log school-house was built at Alexandersville (Alexanderville), and another was erected one and a half miles east of Miamisburg, and was christened 'Gebhart school-house.' The primal church in this Township was also organized at the same place as that of the school-house, and was called the 'Lutheran and Reformed.' The original minister was a Reverend Mr. Dill, a Lutheran.

"Henry Huet (Huiet) raised the first frame house. Miamisburg was originally 'laid out' in the year 1818, by Mr. Stine." (Map from the *Combination Atlas Map of Montgomery County*.)

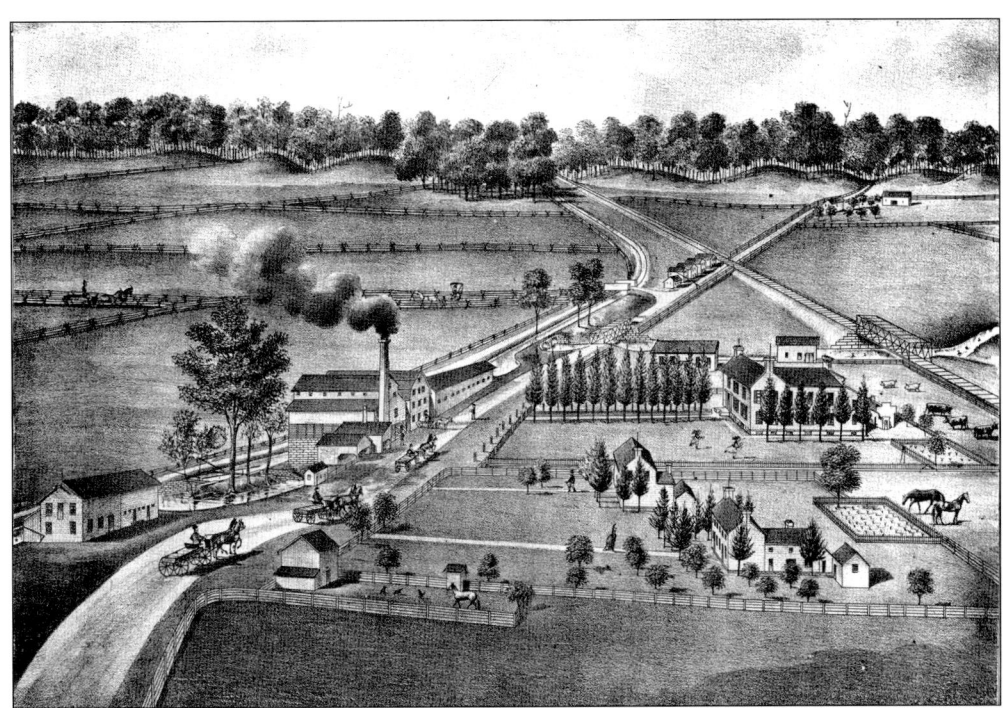

Joseph H. Dryden's farm (above) was located in Section 16, Town One (I) of the township. It was in the northernmost section, just east of the Great Miami River. Today's Dryden Road in the city of Moraine is named for this early farmer, who came to the area in 1837.

The residence of John Poffinbarger (spelled Poffinbaiger on the 1875 map) was in Section 34, at the far northwest corner of the township, west of the Great Miami River. A farmer, he came to the Miamisburg area in 1838. (Drawings from the *Combination Atlas Map of Montgomery County*.)

Built around 1820, this home at 2123 Alex-Bell Road still stands today. It was built by a member of Carrollton's early Pease family and later sold to Valentine Winters, the brother of Reverend David Winters. David's Church (on Mad River and David Roads) is named for the Reverend Winters. Valentine Winters is an ancestor of the Winters banking family and also of Jonathan Winters, the comedian. The home is presently owned by John Kohnle. (Courtesy of Kenneth Hagwood.)

Around 1915, when this photograph was taken, the Cottman-Baker house (at left) on Dayton-Cincinnati Pike was the centerpiece of a working farm. Located in the southwestern corner of the township, the two-story home was built about 1865. In 1995, Miami Township received an historic preservation award from the Ohio Historical Society for the building's restoration after a 1993 fire.

Born in North Carolina in 1796, Samson Strader came to Washington Township (from which Miami Township was carved) in 1804. As a child, he attended Gephart schoolhouse, but more often assisted his family in clearing land to grow corn. He married Mary Benner (also born in 1796), the daughter of Jacob and Mary Benner, in 1817. He purchased land in township Section 22, where he farmed more than 200 acres and built a comfortable home. (Portrait from the *Combination Atlas Map of Montgomery County*.)

The Benner Tavern was built by Jacob Benner in 1813 on a long lane east of what would become Springboro Pike (north of the Miamisburg and Centerville Turnpike). In addition to the tavern, Benner operated a distillery at the site. After his death, his wife Mary spent the rest of her life at the home of her daughter, Mrs. Jonathan Gebhart, who lived on the nearby Gebhart farm in central Miami Township. (Courtesy of Lee Hieronymus.)

The William Turner residence was built in Carrollton (which had been renamed West Carrollton by 1875). A farmer, Turner came to the area in 1820 from Pennsylvania.

RES. OF WILLIAM TURNER
CARROLLTON, MONTGOMERY CO. O.

Dr. J.F. Weist's residence was located in township Section 16. Born in Germany, Dr. Weist (or Wuist) was a physician and surgeon who came to the Alexanderville area (just north of Carrollton) in 1848. (Drawings from the *Combination Atlas Map of Montgomery County*.)

RES. OF DR. J.F. WEIST.
ALEXANDERVILLE, MONTGOMERY CO. O.

22

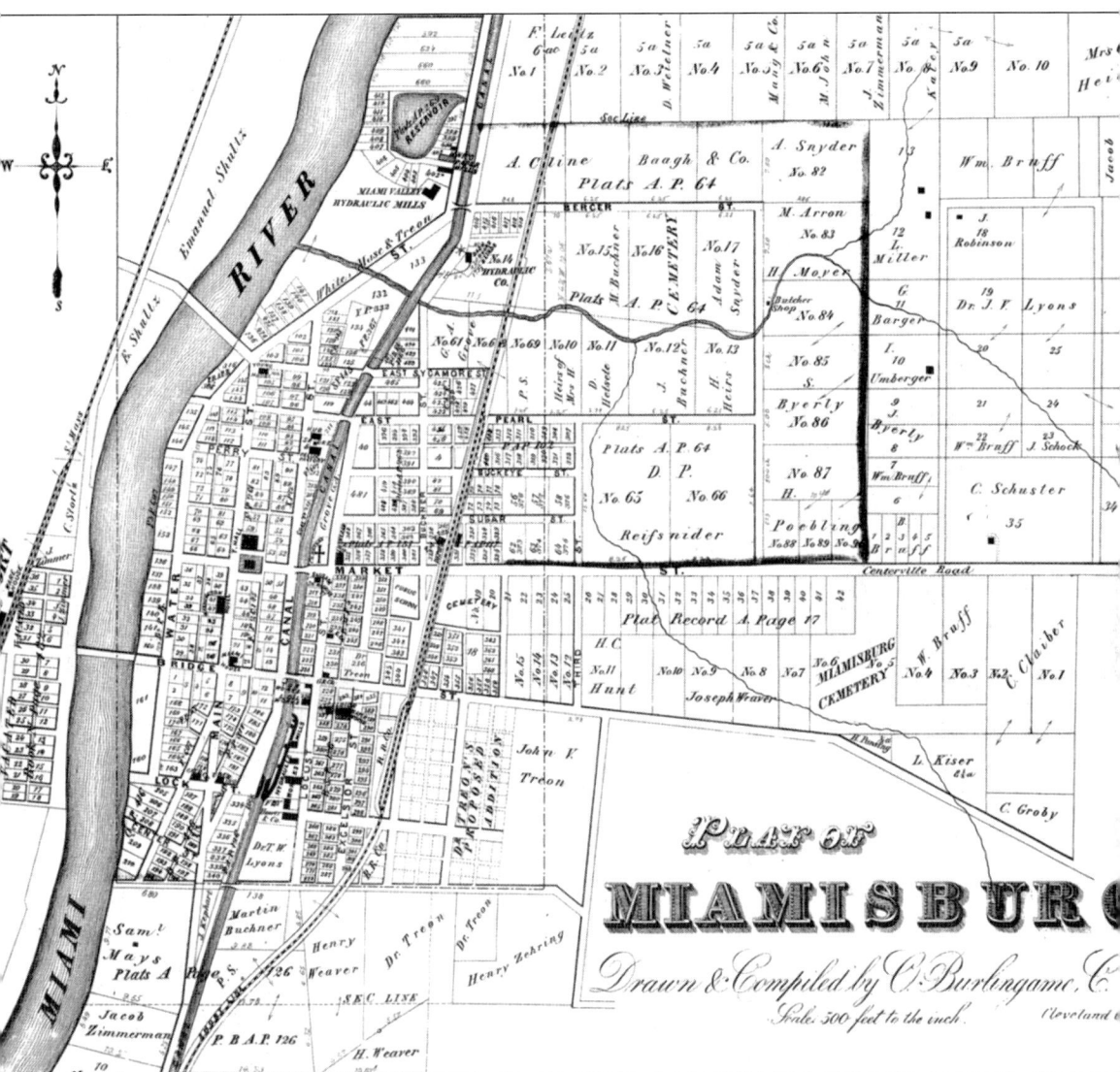

By 1875, the original 1818 Miamisburg plat map had grown from 90 sections to many homes and businesses. West of the river, Bridgeport had warehouses as well as a depot for the Cincinnati, Hamilton, and Dayton (CH&D) railroad.

In Miamisburg, on the east side of the river, there were paper mills, hydraulic mills, and a depot for the Short Line railroad. There was a town hall, churches, public schools, and cemeteries. The Washington Hotel and the Miami House had opened their doors. Businesses included a sash door and blinds factory, a hub and spoke factory, and the Excelsior paper factory. There was a butcher shop east of the town and a sausage machine factory downtown.

Miamisburg had become a town, while Miami Township, to the east and the west, remained mainly a rural area. Still, even in Miamisburg, boys could fish on the banks of the river or in Sycamore and Bear Creeks. Young people went barefoot in the summer and swam in Sycamore Creek near the sash and blind factory. Locust trees bloomed downtown, and the Miami and Erie Canal passed through the center of town. (Map from the *Combination Atlas Map of Montgomery County*.)

Dr. John Treon, a physician and surgeon, arrived in the Miamisburg area in 1811. Born in Pennsylvania, he was only 21 when he and his uncle, Dr. Peter Treon, headed west. They arrived in the area to find only three cabins in Hole's Station: those of Philip Gephart, Daniel Gephart, and Jacob Kercher.

The young doctors bought one of the 10-acre lots, erected a house, farmed, hunted, and practiced medicine until they, along with Kercher and Emanuel Gebhart, laid out Miamisburg's first plat in 1818. As the town's population increased, so did the doctors' practice. They continued as partners for 22 years, when they dissolved their practice by mutual consent.

At the age of 28, Dr. John Treon married Eve Weimar, the daughter of a local farmer. Their marriage lasted more than 54 years before she passed away from heart disease. In 1873, he married Mrs. Elizabeth Black, a widow whom he had known for many years.

After 60 years as a physician, he gave up his practice—but was able to look back on a long, active life. In his early 20s, he had served as a surgeon under General William Hull in the War of 1812. His medical practice had ranged as far east as Zanesville, Ohio, and included patients in Cincinnati, eastern Indiana, and the Lake Erie area.

In addition to his medical practice, over the years he engaged in farming, real estate, and trading in stock and produce. In addition to his residence on East Linden Avenue (built in the 1830s over a three-year period, and still standing today), he owned a large amount of property in the Miamisburg area, several farms in the Miami River valley, and stock in the Hydraulic Water Works, grist mill, and cutlery works.

He died in 1887 at the age of 96. On his monument at Hill Grove Cemetery is carved a picture of his face, looking westward—just as he had done many years earlier, when he made his decision to travel west to the Miami Valley. (Drawings from the *Combination Atlas Map of Montgomery County*.)

Aaron Gebhart (1839–1916) and his wife Sarah Leis Gebhart (1841–1900) lived on a quarter section of land in central Miami Township (the site of today's Holiday Inn). Aaron was the third Gebhart to farm the property; his grandfather John and father Jonathan preceded him. Primarily a tobacco farmer, Aaron and a hired hand also grew other crops. The original Gebhart residence was torn down in 1917 to build a more modern house. Aaron and Sarah had two children, Edna and Harold, each of whom inherited half the farm. The daughter of Harold Gebhart and Nancy Byers was Harriet Gebhart. She married Ted Hieronymus, and the last family member moved from the homesite in 1980. (Courtesy of Lee Hieronymus.)

The Fred C. Fox family arrived in the area in 1809 and began farming in Section 11, Town Two (II) in the southeastern section of the township. Over the years, their children married the children of other pioneer families, including the Gebharts and the Eagles. By 1904, the Fox family had grown so large that their annual family reunion was held at the Montgomery County fairgrounds in Dayton. (Courtesy of *The Miamisburg/West Carrollton News*, Mrs. Jack Fox photograph.)

From 1868 through 1969, township government was conducted at the Miami Township Building located at 19 East Central Avenue in Miamisburg (at the northeast corner of old Market Square). The building was more than a century old when it was sold at auction. It was torn down in 1970. (Courtesy of the Miamisburg Historical Society.)

Three
20TH CENTURY PROGRESS
1900–1959

By the year 1900, the Miami Township area had experienced a century of change and progress. The township's population, including Miamisburg and West Carrollton, had grown to 7,791. Miamisburg, the largest town in Montgomery County, had absorbed Bridgeport, west of the river. Carrollton had changed its name to West Carrollton because another town in eastern Ohio had the same name. It would consolidate with Alexanderville in 1943 and withdraw from the township by 1967.

The area's rural tradition was still strong with tobacco as the staple or "money" crop, but business, small and large, was under way. There were restaurants and general stores, banks, barbershops, and bakeries. West Carrollton was known for its paper mills, Miamisburg for its carriage, binder twine, and cordage factories.

In Miamisburg, businesses were centered around Market and Main streets, and in West Carrollton, around the Union Block and Stine buildings on Central Avenue and Elm Street. In the central township area, small businesses were concentrated along Miamisburg-Centerville Road and Springboro Pike and in an area in the northern part of the township that came to be known as "Moraine City."

At the turn of the century, there were 13 school districts and four schoolhouses in Miami Township. Area students were also educated at public elementary and high schools in Miamisburg and West Carrollton. The first Catholic grade school (St. Joseph's) had opened in Miamisburg in 1890. By 1901, it was known as Our Lady of Good Hope School.

Although a police department for the growing township wasn't organized until the mid-1950s, the fire department was formed in October 1946. The first firemen and equipment were housed in a Miamisburg fire station. The township road department has a much longer history of service to residents. Its employees performed a variety of duties, ranging from the maintenance of roads to vehicle maintenance in a garage located on Miamisburg-Springboro Road.

A major factor in the development of the township and its neighboring towns was their location on the Great Miami River, the natural transportation route between Cincinnati (the metropolis for the entire region) and Dayton and points north.

The *Beers History of Dayton and Montgomery County*, published in the early 1900s, commented on the township's geography: "The Miami River passes through the township, taking a southwesterly course. The most important small streams entering the Miami River, in Miami Township, are Hole's Creek from the east and Bear Creek from the west. Five bridges cross the Miami in the township: one near Alexanderville, one at West Carrollton, two in Miamisburg, and one in the southern part of the township."

The Great Flood of 1913 damaged the bridges as well as the towns along the river. In West Carrollton, the river inundated the entire town except for an island between Pease and Main, near Smith Street. In Miamisburg, Miami Avenue suffered the worst damage, but the river rose to 11 feet on Main and First streets and to nine feet on Second Street.

Other "milestone" events also touched the lives of township residents in the first half of the 20th century.

Miamisburg has been known as the "Star City" since early in its history. The origin of the name is uncertain, but it may refer to the fact that at one time Miamisburg was a center of industry and housed within its city limits industries known far and wide. About 1910, Bert Garrison and his family posed for this photograph in front of their Star City Dairy wagon. (Courtesy of Julia Shupert Hagwood.)

Zion Lutheran Church held a picnic at Benner's Woods off Springboro Pike in the early 1900s. In addition to the pastor, Reverend M.L. Baum (at right), the group included members of the Miller, Caldwell, Long, Weaver, Durst, Crosby, Gebhart, Christman, Henger, Lohman, Froem, Krietzer, Lesher, Holman, Emert, Albrecht, Shell, Degler, Yoe, Stein, Woodman, Benner, Shade, Moser, Holbert, Strader, Peters, Routsong, Winterhalter, Getter, Rich, and McLain families. (Courtesy of Zion Evangelical Lutheran Church.)

With much of Miami Township, from the Miami Shores area of today's Moraine in the north to Chautauqua in the south, located along the Great Miami River, residents soon learned how to deal with spring flooding (above). An early 1900s flood left Dayton-Cincinnati Pike (a former stagecoach and omnibus route along the river) under water, making travel difficult on this major north-south roadway. (Courtesy of the Mote family, Huston Beals photographs.)

This 1926 aerial picture of Miamisburg was sent to customers by the Rike-Kumler Company of Dayton. It was one of a series of 46 photographs taken of cities and towns in the Miami Valley and was used during the company's 73rd anniversary celebration. "We have the ambition and hope of being of real service, not only to the city of Dayton but to all the surrounding territory," said the letter, signed by company president Frederick Rike, which accompanied the photograph. "We are striving to maintain an institution in which you may take a real pride and in which you may find your shopping comfortable, pleasant and profitable."

Included with the letter was a short history of Miamisburg, entitled "A Tobacco Center of High Rank—A Community of Ideals." According to the history, in 1926 Miamisburg had 3,900 residents and three schools that housed 1,200 students and 50 teachers.

At that time, the history said, there were four banks: First National Bank, Farmers & Merchants National Bank, Mutual Building & Loan Co., and Miamisburg Building & Loan Co. Local organizations included the Rotary Club, the Business Men's Club, the Retail Merchants' Association, and an American Legion post. There were two Boy Scout troops too. The Thirkield Co. was the leading dry goods store, and the Suttman Clothing Co. was the leading men's shop. (Courtesy of Esther Light, Rike-Kumler Company photograph.)

Members of the Fox family were clustered in the southeastern section of the township, with farms located on both sides of Swamp Road (today's Spring Valley Pike). In 1875, Fred and Alex Fox owned land in Town II, Section 10; George and A. Fox farmed in Section 15. A winter day in the early 1900s found Fox family members and young Huston Beals enjoying the snow. (Courtesy of the Mote family.)

This 1931 family photograph was taken outside the Cottman-Baker farmhouse on Dayton-Cincinnati Pike. When the two-story home was built, it was customary to construct a summer kitchen separate from the main house. The township hopes to make the restored 1865 home the centerpiece of a transportation heritage park commemorating the river, the Miami and Erie Canal, and the early highway system.

For years, the Siebenthaler Nursery operated a tree farm and nursery in rural Miami Township at the corner of Springboro Pike and Alex-Bell Road. The company's Moraine locust trees, planted in front of many homes along Stroop Road and in the area called Huber South, were grown in rows at the "south" nursery site. Plowing at the township nursery was done by horses; at the nursery's site north of Dayton, mules did the plowing.

The nursery was a family operation. Pictured in the mid-1930s with one of the south site's horses were the Siebenthalers and the Wilsons (Mary Siebenthaler was married to Howard Wilson). (Courtesy of Robert Siebenthaler.)

The Dayton-Wright Airplane Company was formed in 1917 by Col. Edward Deeds and Charles Kettering to manufacture warplanes for World War I. An experimental station located east of the main plant was the company's research and development section. Among its projects were a number of "firsts," including a guided missile. Deeds left the company shortly after its formation to accept a wartime appointment in Washington, D.C. (Courtesy of Special Collections and Archives, Wright State University.)

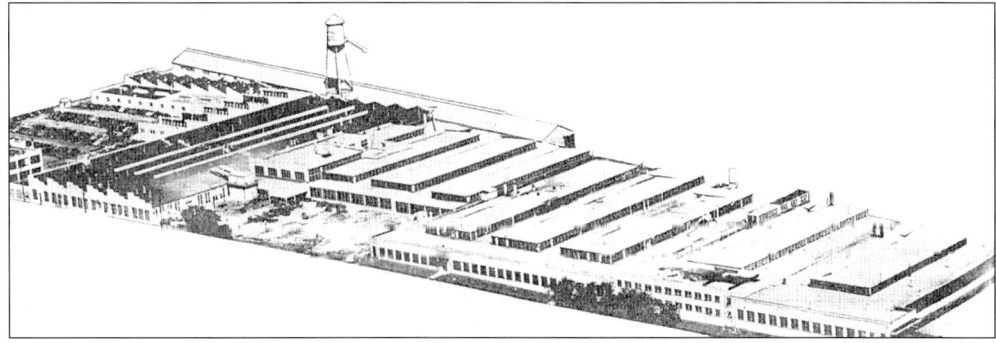

In 1921, General Motors brought its Frigidaire division to an industrial area of Miami and Van Buren Townships known as "Moraine City." During World War II, the facility produced aircraft parts and components. After the war, the plant resumed production of refrigerators. In the 1970s, GM sold the Frigidaire division and later converted the plant to the manufacture of small trucks and automotive components. (Courtesy of Special Collections and Archives, Wright State University.)

MIAMI SHORES
along the Miami River
Playgrounds of MIAMI VALLEY

real place to have a Summer Cottage
a lot with graveled roadways and elec-
icity; beautiful parkways and public dock-
g places.

FULL SIZE LOTS
$95 PER LOT AND UP

One and Two Dollars Weekly
INTEREST OR TAXES FOR ONE YEAR
AFTER PURCHASE

ing your picnic baskets, bathing suits and
hing tackle and have a good time. Good
inking water, benches, tables and chairs.

HOW TO GET THERE

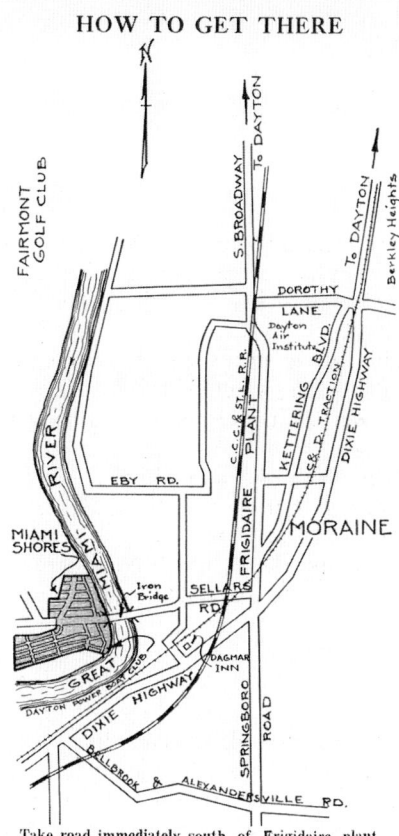

Take road immediately south of Frigidaire plant.

MIAMI SHORES
The Playgrounds of Miami Valley

FULL SIZE LOTS

ALONG THE MIAMI RIVER, WEST OF T
MORAINE FRIGIDAIRE PLANT

BOATING - BATHING - FISHIN

Take a Dip

In a natural swimming pool, fed by sprin
water and surrounded by large forest tree
and a beautiful lawn.

See the Power Boat Racing on the Rive

(*Opposite*) The Miami Shores area, located along the Great Miami River in what was once the northernmost past of Miami Township, was originally advertised as a summer resort: "the playgrounds of the Miami Valley." It offered inexpensive lots (at $95 and up), boating, bathing, fishing, and other vacation activities.

The Dayton Power Boat Club sponsored boat races on the river. There were tree-shaded lawns and a swimming pool fed by spring water. The plat offered electricity, gravel roads, and public docks—all for $1 or $2 a week. Miami Shores was a convenient place for Dayton-area residents to build a summer cottage.

During World War II, however, when production at the "Moraine City" industrial complex was booming and housing was hard to find, people began buying the summer homes for year-round use because no other housing was available.

By the time the war ended, Miami Shores had become a place where residents lived 12 months of the year. "It was a country-like place, a wonderful place to live," according to one family that moved from Dayton to Miami Shores in the late 1940s.

According to Marie Fuller, "It was like a little town. This was originally farmland (the Apple family had owned Section 19 in this part of the township as far back as 1875). There were fruit trees, walnut trees, lots of squirrels." It was a place where children could roam—and nearby on Venetian Way was an old canal where they also could swim.

A civic association, formed in 1949, put together an "active project" list to improve "the Shores" from a vacation campground to a modern residential area. The first projects on the list, streetlights and the construction of a walkway across the Great Miami River bridge in the plat, were completed within a year.

"All the roads out here were two-lane," said Harry Fuller. "They were old gravel roads, and there were no streetlights. You can imagine how dark it was with no streetlights."

The civic association's future agendas included the installation of natural gas in the community's homes, installation of four-way stop signs, and rebuilding the riverbank. In the early 1950s, the association asked the Montgomery County commissioners and the Miami Conservancy District to build a levee to control the flooding problems along the river.

The last big flood in Miami Shores was in January 1959. At the Fuller house, the water was 36 inches deep in the ground-level basement. "We put the freezer up on blocks," said Marie Fuller, "and the water tipped the freezer over. The water also got into our coal furnace. I called the Conservancy District and told them, 'We're not in any danger, but our fire—our furnace—has gone out.'

"A rowboat came right up to the steps below our door to rescue us. On our street, water covered the mailboxes, which were on posts at the street—but the next street over didn't have any water" at all.

Shortly after that flood, the Conservancy District approved flood protection for Miami Shores. A number of houses were moved away from the river and a levee was built. By the 1960s, the area was safe behind an earthworks levee, protected from the rising waters of the Great Miami River. (Courtesy of Harry and Marie Fuller.)

The Miami Township Gravel Plant (above) was still in operation in the 1930s. For years, the township's Road Department crushed local gravel to surface miles of area roads.

Pictured cutting a new road at Richard Street (at Heincke Road in Miamisburg) during the 1930s was a group of Road Department workers, including Harold Paff and Arthur Good and one of the township trustees, Simon Recher. (Courtesy of the Mote family, Huston Beals photographs.)

As part of the "new deal" program after the Great Depression of 1929, relief workers were hired to help build roads in the township. Road Department trucks transported the workers to the job site. The workers received no monetary wages, but were given groceries and coal to heat their homes as payment for their road building efforts. (Courtesy of the Mote family, Huston Beals photograph.)

During World War II, the scrap metal collected at the Road Department garage on Miamisburg-Springboro Road was used as the township's "homefront" contribution to the war effort. (Courtesy of the Mote family, Huston Beals photograph.)

The Miami Township Fire Department was formed in 1946. At that time, firemen and equipment were housed at existing stations in Miamisburg and West Carrollton. Fire Station No. 1 was located in the same building as the Miamisburg Fire Department. Two different signals were used to notify the firefighters: one blast on the whistle for Miamisburg fires and an oscillating tone for fires in the township.

Shortly after the formation of a township Fire Department, a ladies' auxiliary, composed primarily of the firefighters' wives, was organized. Members of this group, photographed in the 1940s, met regularly for social and fund-raising activities. (Courtesy of Huston Beals.)

Before the Police Department was formed in the 1950s, the only form of law enforcement in the township was a one-man volunteer constable system. The original police station was located at the site of today's Fire Station 48: Jomar Avenue and Springboro Pike. Thirty years later, trustees Berman Layer and Shirley Omietanski and clerk-treasurer Frank Cleary joined Police Chief James Moore at the groundbreaking for today's police station.

During the 1960s, the Police Department had only three patrol cars and a patrol boat to use on the Great Miami River. Over the years, because of increased demand for services and a greater number of full-time officers, the department moved its headquarters into larger sites on Miamisburg-Centerville Road and at the township administrative offices on Lyons Road before building a new facility at 2660 Lyons Road in 1987.

South Field, the private airfield of Col. Edward Deeds, was located at his estate, Moraine Farm, on Stroop Road in Miami and Van Buren Townships. In 1928, he purchased the first luxury airplane manufactured in the U.S., an all-metal 10-passenger Ford Tri-Motor. When not in use, the airplane was parked at the landing pad on the airfield.

The Experimental Station of the Dayton-Wright Airplane Company was also located at the airfield, east of the Dayton-Wright Airplane Company. The nation's first guided missile was developed at the Experimental Station in 1918 under the direction of Charles Kettering, who headed the research and development section of the company. The missile, called the *Bug*, was a predecessor of the German World War II buzz bomb.

In *A Field Guide to Flight: On the Aviation Trail in Dayton, Ohio*, Mary Ann Johnson described the *Bug* as "a small robot biplane designed to act as an aerial torpedo." Its yellow poplar propeller was designed by Orville Wright, the consulting engineer to the Dayton-Wright Airplane Company. Its four-cylinder, 40-horsepower engine was designed by noted race car driver Ralph DePalma and former Ford Motor Car Company engineer C.H. Wills.

After World War I ended, Col. Deeds continued his association with aviation. He helped form the Pratt and Whitney Aircraft Company in 1925 and served as a director of Pan American Airways starting in 1931. He is probably best known for his partnership with Charles Kettering (which led to the formation of Dayton Engineering Laboratories Company/DELCO) and for his long career at the National Cash Register Company.

At one time, the Moraine Farm property totaled 600 acres. Today, only a few acres surrounding Col. Deeds' residence remain. It is presently owned by the NCR Corporation, which maintains the property as a guesthouse and meeting place. A Huber Homes development now occupies 125 acres of what was once Col. Deeds' private airport. (Courtesy of Huston Beals.)

Four
THE "URBAN" TOWNSHIP
1960–1980

Still a rural area in the 1950s, today's Miami Township is an "urban" township, unlike most townships in the state of Ohio. Other townships tend to encompass rural areas, but since the 1960s, Miami Township has been home to scores of businesses, both retail and industrial.

The change occurred gradually in the 1950s and early 1960s. It started with the construction of "plats" of new homes on township farmland and a former airfield. More farmland disappeared as the interstate highway system was expanded, with ramps providing access to the central portion of the township, as well as to the neighboring cities of Miamisburg and West Carrollton.

Then came the Dayton Mall, in 1969, and the growth mushroomed. Located at the intersection of Miamisburg-Centerville Road (State Route 725) and Springboro Pike (State Route 741), "the Mall" soon became a cornerstone of retail activity in the township, as well as the entire southwest Dayton region. For years, the Dayton Mall was the township's largest employer. Today it is joined by National City Mortgage, Lexis-Nexis, and Metropolitan Life.

Farmland also disappeared as a result of annexations by neighboring cities. In April 1965, for example, after an 80-acre annexation from Miami Township, the village of Moraine was declared a city. The annexation gave Moraine a population of 5,455—just 455 more than the 5,000 minimum population required for city status. A later annexation from northern Miami Township added 63.9 acres, 249 properties, 376 property owners, and an estimated population of 700 to the city of Moraine.

Over the years, annexations have reduced the township from 40 square miles to less than 25 square miles in size. Still, areas of green space remain, and there is a strong effort to keep it that way.

The township's administrator, trustees, and Planning and Zoning Department know that most of the rural areas are gone, and they won't come back. But the township continues its 30-year commitment to control development by determining the best locations for parks, business, industry, and residential development in the rapidly growing township and to ensure the "good life" for Miami Township residents.

In the 1970s, a number of businesses wanted to move into the area around the Dayton Mall. Residents were concerned that businesses might become their next-door neighbors. They were concerned about the traffic already generated on over-strained roads—and about the traffic yet to come. Efforts to keep the township from continuing in the pattern of urban sprawl began in 1971 and led to home rule zoning for Miami Township in 1972.

Township officials and residents decided that a land-use plan would be an effective tool for controlling development, so the Miami Valley Regional Planning Commission was contracted in 1975 to complete a plan. The first in a series of citizen input meetings was held that November, and more than 1,000 residents attended it. The business, the sprawl, the traffic were, indeed, what concerned them. They said so at the meeting.

Principles of the land-use plan developed as a result of those meetings are still followed today.

"Modern Manor," a planned development of single-family homes, was built on Col. Edward Deeds' former airfield in the mid-1950s. The plan called for 2,000 ranch-style brick homes to be built in northern Miami Township between 1954 and 1956.

The plat's developer was the Huber Construction Company, which also built homes northeast of Dayton (today's Huber Heights) and apartment buildings along Far Hills Avenue in Kettering.

The name "Modern Manor" failed to catch on, and today the neighborhood is known as Huber South. Parts of the development have been annexed by the neighboring city of Moraine; the remainder still lies within the boundaries of Miami Township. (Courtesy of Theresa Huber, Marion Rife photograph.)

The Huber South development extended south from Stroop Road to Bushwick Avenue. It was located just a few blocks east of the Moraine City industrial complex that included Frigidaire and other General Motors operations. Sidewalks were built throughout the plat, and a Moraine locust tree (grown nearby at Siebenthaler Nursery) was planted in front of each home.

Houses in Huber South were popular with young families. Former University of Dayton and NBA basketball player Jim Paxson Sr. was photographed outside his family's Huber home in 1956. (Courtesy of Theresa Huber, Marion Rife photographs.)

The Moraine City elementary school was named for the industrial complex located between Dixie Highway and Springboro Pike on the border of Miami and Moraine (formerly Van Buren) townships.

After World War II ended, the Moraine City industrial plants resumed production, and an influx of workers and their families arrived in the area. Many who were looking for well-paying factory jobs found what they were seeking here. They built small homes on land nearby, renovated the summer homes in Miami Shores, or moved their families into one of several mobile home parks in the area.

In 1952, Van Buren Township voters supported the formation of a village called Kettering. Three months later, however, a majority of the residents in the southwestern sector of the new village (today's Moraine) voted for detachment from Kettering.

The newly formed Moraine Township included 2,250 acres of land, the GM Frigidaire plant, and a number of commercial businesses. Its 665 registered voters lived in homes east and west of the Frigidaire plant, or on farms and mobile home parks north of the industrial area. Located to the south and southeast of the new township was Miami Township.

Detachment from Kettering did not separate Moraine from the Kettering and West Carrollton school districts. The children who lived in Moraine continued to attend school in these neighboring communities.

Moraine City School (today's C.F. Holliday School) on South Dixie Drive was (and still is) part of the West Carrollton School District. In 1956, when this picture was taken, Mrs. Mildred Gilbert's third and fourth grade students lived in Moraine, as well as in the new Huber South area of Miami Township. (Courtesy of the West Carrollton Historical Society.)

Rows of thornless Moraine locust trees and other trees and plants once filled Siebenthaler Nursery's "south" operations at the northeast corner of Springboro Pike and Alex-Bell Road. Many of the nursery's customers lived in the new plats of brick homes being built on former farmland east and west of Springboro Pike.

On the grounds of the nursery complex, hidden by the trees, was a cabin used for special functions by Siebenthaler workers—and by township and West Carrollton residents. When the land became too valuable to continue to be used as a nursery, it was put up for sale, and the cabin was moved to the nursery's "north" location. (Courtesy of Robert Siebenthaler.)

Springboro Pike was still a two-lane country road when Shirley Omietanski's family, the Griesmeyers, took this picture in 1938. The rural township's population explosion began in the mid-1950s and early 1960s when farmers began selling their land to developers who built hundreds of homes on both sides of Springboro Pike. (Courtesy of Shirley Omietanski.)

Also located on rural Springboro Pike, south of Miamisburg-Centerville Road, was the home where Peggy Fox Geer grew up. Miles Fox, her father, was a descendent of Miami Township's early Fox family, as well as the Gebharts and the Eagles, two of the township's pioneer families. As a child, Miles Fox attended Miami Township District School 13, where his seventh grade teacher (in 1914) was Anna K. Wantz. (Courtesy of Peggy Fox Geer.)

Springboro Pike's growth over the past 40 years is evident in this 1965 aerial photograph of St. Henry Parish (above) and its school, rectory, and convent. Since that time, a church and a parish activity center have been built on the parish grounds, and Cox Arboretum and Gardens, part of the Five Rivers MetroParks System, has grown from farmland into 189 acres of attractive buildings, natural wooded areas, and specialty gardens. (Courtesy of St. Henry Parish.)

An increase in new homes and in the school-age population resulted in the construction of LaVeta Bauer elementary school on Springboro Pike just south of Cox Arboretum in 1967. James Oren taught Bauer sixth graders from 1968 until the mid-1990s when the Miamisburg School District moved all its middle-school students to Neff and Wantz Schools. This picture of Mr. Oren and his students was taken in the early 1980s. (Courtesy of Tim Oren.)

When the Dayton Mall was built in 1969, township growth mushroomed. Located southeast of the Miamisburg-Centerville Road and Springboro Pike intersection, "the Mall" soon became a cornerstone of retail activity in the township.

Shoppers from around the Dayton region were attracted to the completely enclosed complex that featured three "flagship" stores: JC Penney, Sears, and Rike's (later Lazarus and today Lazarus-Macy's). For years, the Mall's 100+ stores made it the township's largest employer.

Over the past 30 years, the Mall has grown in size, both inside and out. A fourth flagship store, Elder-Beerman, was added in the 1990s, along with a new wing built on the north side of the complex.

To keep the shopping center "family friendly," a new weekend policy was initiated in 2003. On Friday and Saturday evenings, all shoppers under the age of 16 must be accompanied by a parent or other adult. The MB-16 policy earned the township Police Department and Michael Minns, the Mall's general manager, a 2004 Crime Prevention Project of the Year award from the Ohio Crime Prevention Association. (Courtesy of Dayton Mall General Manager Michael Minns.)

When it first opened, the Dayton Mall offered two stories of shopping and 115 stores under one roof. There were movie theaters and music stores, a bookstore and a bridal boutique, shoe stores and a sewing center, as well as a bank, a candy store, and a drugstore. Weary shoppers could visit a restaurant, a snack bar, or a pizza place. Over the years, regular renovations have updated the Mall's appearance. Today it features new skylights, signage, and a glass-walled elevator, as well as a second floor Café Court with plenty of chairs, tables, and food of every description. (Courtesy of Dayton Mall General Manager Michael Minns.)

Construction of an Interstate 75 interchange in central Miami Township during the mid-1960s turned much of the Hieronymus farm (the former Gebhart farm) at the southwest corner of Miamisburg-Centerville Road and Springboro Pike into paved I-75 access ramps and a future business district. Construction supplies were stacked in the fields (above); bridge supports for Lyons Road were erected across the former farmland. (Courtesy of Lee Hieronymus.)

Groundbreaking ceremonies for Bush-Dell Park (today's Layer Park) in the Huber South neighborhood took place in 1973. The seven-acre park was developed at the corner of Bushwick and Cordell Drives on land purchased from Siebenthaler Nursery and the Miami Valley Hunt & Polo Club. Intended to serve as a neighborhood park, it was equipped with two basketball courts, a softball diamond, a picnic area, an open play area, and a tot lot. (Courtesy of Paul Tucker.)

Miami View Park was also developed in 1973 on a 20-acre site located on Munger Road. Envisioned as a community park to serve large segments of the township, it included both level and rolling wooded terrain. In addition to a small lake for fishing, it was equipped with four tennis courts, two basketball courts, baseball and softball diamonds, a shelter house with restrooms, a picnic area, biking trails, an amphitheater, roads, and parking lots.

Waldruhe Park, whose name means "Forest rest," was donated to the city of Dayton (and later to the township) by Adam Schantz in 1917. More than 50 acres in size, the former site of the Schantz summer cottage is located on Springboro Pike, south of the Dayton Mall. At a ceremony attended by Schantz's daughter, Gertrude Schantz Weng (at left of rock), the township dedicated a plaque to honor the family whose gift is still appreciated. (Courtesy of Berman Layer.)

For more than 85 years, Waldruhe Park has offered its visitors the opportunity to hike on nature trails and view migrating birds, wildflowers, and majestic oak trees that are hundreds of years old. To ensure that Waldruhe would retain its natural setting, for years its facilities were limited to two open-air picnic shelters and a horseshoe pit. (Courtesy of Paul Tucker.)

To celebrate Miami Township's 150th anniversary in 1979, a ceremony was held to dedicate this historical marker commemorating the Sunfish Lock (Lock 27) on the Miami and Erie Canal. Curtis Eagle (behind the sign) grew up on a farm down the road and as a boy, fished in the canal. Other participants included Berman Layer (at right), township officials, and Boy Scouts, who had raised the flag to open the festivities at Crains Run Park. (Courtesy of Berman Layer.)

The township's 150th anniversary celebration included a parade through the Singing Hills neighborhood (east of Springboro Pike) to Miami View Park, where a children's carnival was held. Additional events, including reenactments and pioneer games (such as tomahawk throwing) with members of the Simon Kenton Long Rifles, a fife and drum corps, and a "float-in" by Shelby County canoeists, were held at Crains Run Park. (Courtesy of Paul Tucker.)

Groundbreaking for a new Miami Township building at 2700 Lyons Road took place in 1969. Members of the Fire and Police Departments looked on as participants in the ceremony, including clerk-treasurer Gerald Malott and trustees Barney Grooms, William McCabe, and Oscar Page, shared a ceremonial shovel. Built on land originally owned by the Woods family, the government center opened in 1970 and was enlarged 10 years later.

In 1970, the township's government center included offices for the trustees, clerk-treasurer, and other officials. For years, the building also served as Police Headquarters. Today, the facility houses administrative offices, as well as the Planning and Zoning, Finance, and Human Resources Departments, a conference room, a training room, and a trustees' meeting room. Fire Headquarters and Station 50 are located at the west end of the building.

Five
FROM FOOTPATHS TO AIRPORTS
1797–1960

The earliest residents of today's Miami Township arrived by water (along the Great Miami River), or by land (on footpaths leading to this fertile river valley). A major factor in the development of the township was its location on the natural transportation route between Cincinnati and the confluence of the Great Miami and Mad Rivers, at the site that was to become Dayton.

The first footpaths in the area were replaced by rough roads in the late 1700s and early 1800s. The river, however, was always there—although the means of traveling on it changed over the years.

Predating the formation of Miami Township was the Miami and Erie Canal. It was authorized in February 1825, and construction began in June 1827. On December 22, 1827, the packet *Alpha* traveled the canal from Dayton through Carrollton to Miamisburg. By January 1829, the canal was completed to within four miles of Cincinnati. River commerce was changing from keelboat to canal boat.

Soon after the canal was completed, however, it was obsolete. The era of the "iron horse" was dawning. In 1851, the CH&D (Cincinnati, Hamilton, and Dayton) railroad line began operation through stations in Carrollton and Miamisburg. The "Big Four" railroad was built in 1872.

The era of the toll roads was between 1830 and 1870, with toll houses located at equal distances. Toll fees were 3¢ for a horse and rider, 6¢ for an empty wagon, and 12¢ for a loaded wagon. The proceeds were used for the upkeep of the roads: another layer of gravel.

Several turnpike companies were chartered to build macadamized roads connecting Cincinnati and other towns. One of these was the Great Miami Turnpike, constructed in 1840, which was later known as Dixie Highway and U.S. Route 25.

The development of the interurban electric railroad, which promised to revolutionize passenger, freight, and express transportation, began about 1895. The Dayton Traction Co. between Dayton and Miamisburg opened on July 1, 1896. Two years later, Dayton and Cincinnati were linked by trolley lines through West Carrollton.

The big red traction cars provided safe, clean, fast, and inexpensive transportation. By the 1940s, however, the last traction car had gone through the township area. Motor buses provided more modern transportation, so the traction lines were removed to make way for a two-lane highway.

The 20th century saw major advances in transportation, which resulted in major changes in Miami Township itself. The invention of powered flight resulted in the construction of three airfields (and a seaplane base) at various locations in the township. Mass production of automobiles in the early 1900s diminished residents' reliance on horses, trains, and buses as forms of transportation.

By the 1960s, two or more cars were parked in many garages and driveways—or causing congestion on township streets. As traffic increased throughout the area, interstate highway systems were constructed, and access ramps were built over fertile Miami Township farmland. The first footpaths had been paved; much of the farmland had disappeared; and only the river remained as a reminder of an earlier era.

According to Dr. George Knepper, in *The Official Ohio Lands Book*, "Canals opened the interior of Ohio to national and world markets. In 1825 the state commenced construction on the Ohio and Erie Canal and the Miami Canal, later extended into the Miami and Erie Canal. It was an enormous undertaking for a relatively poor state to handle. Ohio...sold state-backed bonds in eastern money markets to finance construction of these two through routes connecting Lake Erie with the Ohio River.

"In Ohio's settled areas, land for canal right-of-way was secured through eminent domain. In some cases, land owners donated right-of-way to the state knowing that a canal would enhance the value of their remaining holdings. The northward extension of the Miami and Erie, however, ran largely through unsold federal lands. In 1828, Congress granted Ohio 500,000 acres in the state's northwestern region to help finance the northward extension of the Miami Canal. This was the first of several grants.

"Ohio's canal era was rather brief. Construction started July 4, 1825. The mature canal system had scarcely begun to function when, in the 1850s, large scale railroad development undercut the canals' importance. By encouraging railroad development, the state actually contributed to the demise of its considerable canal investment. In the Civil War era, the state surrendered control of the system to private interests that took what profit they could and allowed the system to deteriorate. In 1913, a great flood washed out or destroyed nearly all the still viable sections."

In Miamisburg, the canal paralleled Main and Locust Streets, with bridges at Pearl, Market, and Bridge Streets. In Carrollton, the canal paralleled Central Avenue, with bridges at Bridge, Elm, and Cedar Streets. At Cedar Street, a high bridge crossed at an angle. This bridge was followed by another, crossing at right angles, which could be raised at one end for the canal boats to pass beneath. (Map from *The Official Ohio Lands Book*.)

The Miami and Erie Canal was authorized in February 1825, and construction began in June 1827. Two years before Miami Township was formed (on December 22, 1827), the packet *Alpha* traveled the canal from Dayton through Carrollton to Miamisburg. In January 1829, the first boats from Cincinnati came through the township on their trip north to Dayton. (Courtesy of Dave Neuhardt.)

A Miamisburg canal lock was located behind the Great Peerless Mills (the site of today's Peerless Mill Inn), which started out as a sawmill in the 1820s. After the Civil War, the sawmill was operated in conjunction with a flour mill. By 1907, the Great Peerless Mills' products included Peerless Flour. The owner's dream, however, was to operate a restaurant. So, in 1929, he converted his mill into an inn and opened the Peerless Pantry. (Courtesy of Mark Renwick, Peerless Mill Inn photograph.)

The canal belonged to a time when life, like the canal, moved slowly. Although the canal was gone by the end of the 19th century, it's said that the manufacturing towns of the Miami Valley are monuments to its existence, for the canal brought industry of many kinds to its banks. In Miamisburg, the "Cinder Path" parking area along First Street was once the canal bed; West Carrollton filled in the canal to form Weidner Park on Central Avenue. (Courtesy of Dave Neuhardt.)

"This (Miamisburg) bridge," says a note on the postcard, "pictures the sleepy laziness of a little town. The cables…are not equalized and one end lifts a little faster than the other, causing it to jam. A young lady lost a quarter through a crack (but) by raising the bridge it could be recovered. An old man…called out the fire department. The bridge stuck and tied up traffic for an hour, and…a small boy crawled under the bridge…got the quarter and kept it." (Courtesy of Mark Renwick.)

The 1840s and 1850s were the heyday of the canal, as it moved the produce of the countryside: bacon, flour, whiskey, beer, pork, corn, coal, and lumber. Sidewheelers and passenger boats, with their awnings shading the decks, long tables for dining, and good bunks, traversed the canal too. Conley Gebhart was the lockkeeper at Miami Township's Sunfish Lock, where he lived in a small frame cabin built along the canal bank. (Courtesy of the Miamisburg Branch Library, Elmer Gaffney print.)

Sunfish Lock (Lock 27) was located across the river from Chautauqua. Over the years, it had deteriorated, but the canal area and lock were restored by Miami Township between 1979 (when the township celebrated its 150th anniversary) and the 1990s. This 1994 picture shows the canal's culvert over Shephard's Run with a bridge abutment from the pre-1920 alignment of the CCC&I Railroad in the foreground. (Courtesy of Kenneth Foster.)

By the time the Miami and Erie Canal was completed, it was obsolete: the era of the railroad had begun. The "Big Four" Railroad, the CCC&I (also known as the "Short Line"), was built in 1852. Its tracks bisected Carrollton and Miamisburg just east of their downtown areas. This train is shown traveling through "the Narrows," east of the Great Miami River near the shared border of the neighboring towns. (Courtesy of the Miamisburg Branch Library, Elmer Gaffney print.)

By 1872, the Cleveland, Columbus, Cincinnati, and Indianapolis Railroad had become an important carrier, purchasing land from the Corporation Cemetery (today's Library Park). The CCC&I (later, the New York Central and the Penn Central) ran on tracks used by today's Norfolk and Southern, which still runs freight trains through Miamisburg and West Carrollton. Miamisburg's Big Four train depot attracted a number of passengers as well as freight. (Courtesy of the Miamisburg Historical Society.)

This picture shows smoke rising from a Big Four Railroad fire in Miamisburg, disrupting nearby foot and vehicle traffic. The busy railroad line also disrupted school classes: students and teachers found it hard to ignore the noise caused by the CCC&I's numerous freight and passenger trains as they rolled by the old brick and frame school buildings at Central Avenue and Third Street (the site of today's Our Lady of Good Hope Church). (Courtesy of Dave Neuhardt.)

In 1851, the CH&D (Cincinnati, Hamilton, and Dayton) Railroad line began operation through stations in Carrollton (later Whitfield) and Miamisburg. Its tracks were located west of the Great Miami River, where this picture shows the train depot under construction. During the 1913 Flood, the depot was carried away downstream. The CH&D line eventually became part of the Baltimore and Ohio (B&O) Railroad. (Courtesy of Julia Shupert Hagwood.)

The Great Miami Turnpike Company, one of several companies that built macadamized roads, was chartered in 1837 "to construct the road from Dayton over the hills long known as the Carrmonte hill (now Kettering), through Miamisburg, Franklin and Middletown, to its junction with the Cincinnati Pike at Sharon."

The Great Miami Turnpike, which was later known as Dixie Highway and U.S. Route 25, was built in 1840. It ran through Miami Township from Chautauqua to the future Moraine City and on to Dayton. This 1918 picture, looking north along the Dixie Highway from Franklin, just south of Chautauqua, shows the road being prepared for levee construction and repaving.

Today's Miamisburg-Centerville Road (SR 725) was originally the Miamisburg-Centerville Pike. It was recorded as a "country road" in 1816, running from Yeazell's Ferry (at the foot of Ferry Street in Miamisburg) to Centerville. By 1827, it had been designated as a state road, although it might have become a turnpike at a later date. Early roads were not much more than a single track filled with ruts, but the turnpike companies converted them to graveled roads and improved them with bridges that crossed creeks.

Another early turnpike in the area was the "southwestern turnpike" or Miamisburg-Springboro Road. The date of its conversion to a "free pike" is unknown, but in 1913, the foundation of the old toll house (which had burned down) was found on Linden Avenue.

The era of the toll roads was between 1830 and 1870. Toll houses were located at equal distances along the roads, and toll-keepers protected against non-payment of the toll by leaning poles across the road. The toll-keeper could raise and lower the poles at will. In Carrollton, a toll house and a milestone were located at the lower end of the Oklahoma area, with another milestone near the school at Cedar Street. (Courtesy of Special Collections and Archives, Wright State University.)

The development of the interurban electric railroad began around 1895. The Dayton Traction Company ran its first traction car between Miamisburg and Dayton in 1896. Two years later, Dayton and Cincinnati were linked by tracks that followed the canal bed down Central Avenue in West Carrollton, with stops at Union Block and other streets.

The big red traction cars pictured above on the Linden Avenue bridge in Miamisburg provided safe (the accident shown below being an exception), clean, fast, and inexpensive transportation. The cars ran every half hour and cost 25¢ for a round trip. Eventually, however, the traction lines were paved over for two-lane highways. (Courtesy of Dave Neuhardt.)

"This rather remarkable photograph was taken at 'the Narrows' just a half-mile north of Miamisburg where the river, canal, interurban and railroad lines and the Cincinnati Pike parallel for a short distance—to our knowledge, the only place in the country where this occurs." The photograph and its explanatory caption were published in *Delco*, dated July 3, 1914.

The site of the photograph, looking north on Dayton-Cincinnati Pike between Miamisburg and West Carrollton, can be visited today, but it no longer looks the same. The Great Miami River (at far left) still parallels the highway, but is hard to see because of the many trees that have matured over the past 100 years.

The interurban electric railroad (second from left), with its traction cars, is gone. In many locations, its lines were paved over to make room for a highway.

The two-lane Dayton-Cincinnati Pike (at center) is no longer a major highway connecting

southwestern Ohio's two largest cities. Today, it's a scenic route between the neighboring cities of West Carrollton (where it's called Central Avenue) and Miamisburg (Main Street).

Traces of the Miami and Erie Canal (near right) can still be seen along the highway. Although much of the canal itself has been filled in, and most landmarks of the canal have disappeared, the canal bed, covered with vegetation, is still visible south of West Carrollton.

The railroad lines, too, remain. Passenger trains no longer serve the area, but freight trains still run through Miamisburg and West Carrollton, just a block or two from the center of each city.

Since this picture was taken in 1914, however, a new form of transportation has been added to "the Narrows": the River Corridor Bikeway, a paved walkway and bicycle path that parallels the river. The area now attracts walkers, joggers, and runners, as well as cyclists and skateboarders. (Courtesy of the Miamisburg Historical Society.)

Air transportation sites have also been located in the township. Col. Edward Deeds' private airfield, South Field (pictured above), was built on his estate near Stroop Road (today's Huber South neighborhood). The Moraine Airpark is located on Clearview Road in a curve of the Great Miami River on land that was once part of Miami Township. The Wright brothers tested the Dayton-Wright Airplane Company's first float plane nearby. (Courtesy of Donald Huber.)

The township has been home to a small airfield, known today as Dayton-Wright Brothers Airport (on Springboro Pike, south of Austin Road), for more than 60 years. Dayton's "Aviation Trail," a self-guided tour of sites associated with Wilbur and Orville Wright, includes a stop at the airport where a replica of the 1911 Wright "B" Flyer is housed in a hangar built to resemble the original Wright hangar on Huffman Prairie. (Courtesy of Paul Tucker.)

Six
Tobacco, Paper, and Nuclear Energy
1800s–1992

In the year 1874, *Township Personals and Directories of Montgomery County* listed more than 100 "principal producers" living in Miami Township who patronized the book. More than half of those listed were farmers; the others were involved in a variety of occupations, ranging from pastors and ministers to teachers, physicians, and surgeons.

Commercial business, too, was under way. There was a dealer in books and stationery, a newspaper publisher, a blacksmith, a contractor and builder, a lumber dealer, and a hotel keeper, as well as manufacturers, dealers in boots and shoes, and a barber and hairdresser.

Businesses were located primarily in the towns of Miamisburg and Carrollton. Farmers still grew crops of many kinds, primarily tobacco, but commerce and services came early to the platted areas. When Miamisburg's first plat was laid out in 1818, the town was already home to the Huiet grist mill (established in 1809), Daniel Gebhart's tavern (1811), and the Treons' medical practice (1811).

In Carrollton, Horatio Phillips, Alexander Grimes, and Moses Smith, the owners of 26 lots, had formed plats in 1839. As early as 1833, however, Horace and Perry Pease had planted an experimental field of tobacco. Then, utilizing power from Carrollton's locks on the Miami and Erie Canal, the Pease brothers established a flour mill and a distillery. They fed the distillery's waste products to hogs—another thriving business developed.

An 1886 composite map of Miamisburg depicts a number of businesses, from attorneys to tobacco buyers. Charles Baum was proprietor of the Star City Opera House, and there were two newspapers: the Blossom brothers published the *Miamisburg Bulletin*, and Charles Kinder published the *Miamisburg News*.

There was Young's Arcade, Kuehn's Brewery, Beiswenger's Bakery, Walborn and Lyon's drug store, Groby & Co.'s bank, Engleman's flour mills, Schuster's saloon and restaurant, Buehner's saloon and restaurant, Wertz & Cade's stoves and tinware, Weaver's groceries and hardware store, Dodds' confectionary and news stand, Clark's dry goods and notions, the Miami House, the Washington House, and the Kress House.

Manufacturing operations included Kauffman Buggy Company, Bookwalter Brothers' Hub and Spoke factory, Excelsior Twine, Binder & Mower works, Miamisburg Binder Twine & Cordage Company, and the Ohio and Miami Valley paper companies.

West Carrollton's early businesses centered around the Union Block building downtown. Shannon's General Store was established there in the 1890s, and groceries were sold in bulk. Small businesses came and went. Among them were the Emerick Barber Shop, Frank Reis' Bakery, Chapman's (later Monbeck's), and King's Shoe Repair.

The first druggist was James Magoteaux, and Francis Nicholas built a livery barn on Smith Street between Central and Main. He kept several horses and provided transportation for various occasions: coaches for funerals, two moving vans, and hansom cabs that seated four passengers.

By the 1870s, the Pease brothers' distillery had been converted into prosperous paper mills. One, the Friend Paper and Tablet Company, later became the Miami Paper Company. Over the years, other paper companies included Karolton Envelope, Bergstrom Paper Company, and the West Carrollton Parchment Company.

Tobacco farming in Miami Township began with the Pease brothers in Carrollton around 1833. Five years later, a farmer named Pomeroy grew the first tobacco crop of any size planted south of Miamisburg. The early settlers soon realized that an acre of tobacco was much more profitable than an acre of wheat or corn.

By 1894, in the township alone, 1,636 acres of tobacco were under cultivation—leading all of Montgomery County in tobacco production. One early tobacco farmer was Christian Schuster, whose home and tobacco plants are pictured above. The photograph of his wife Mary Elizabeth was taken inside their farmhouse. (Courtesy of the Miamisburg Historical Society.)

After the tobacco in the farmer's field was planted, wormed, ripened, and cut, it was dried in his tobacco shed, and then taken to a nearby warehouse for processing. Ganns Tobacco & Leaf was one of the warehouses that processed the tobacco grown on township farms. During packing season, warehouses like Ganns employed both men and women to sort and pack the tobacco leaves.

Although the farmers made money growing tobacco, much more money was made in merchandising (buying and selling the tobacco) and in operating warehouses. It's said that some small fortunes were made by the owners of tobacco warehouses in Miamisburg. (Courtesy of the Miamisburg Branch Library, Elmer Gaffney prints.)

In the days of buggies, spring-wagons, carriages, and surreys, the Enterprise Carriage Factory, a large red brick building in Miamisburg, produced many of these vehicles. At one time, Enterprise was the largest factory in the village. Although known far and wide, it existed in Miamisburg for only 27 years.

One of Esther Light's essays (in *Miamisburg: The Story of Our Town*) tells the story of the carriage factory. In the spring of 1890, the Enterprise Buggy Company (then located in Cincinnati) was invited to relocate in Miamisburg. Ground for the new plant was furnished by the village near the "Big Four" railroad tracks between Pearl and Sycamore Streets. The building would include 136,000 square feet of floor space, would be four stories high, and would employ between 300 and 350 men.

When Enterprise moved to Miamisburg, it was turning out 800 vehicles a year. Before it closed, it turned out more than 15,000 a year; and by 1912 it was said to have a capacity for manufacturing 25,000.

Early in 1891, the building was completed, machinery moved or purchased, and manufacturing operations began. The factory was one of the most complete carriage plants in the country—certainly the most up-to-date, with fireproof doors, elevators installed by a local machinist, plus a battery of boilers, and a large engine.

While a line of high-class vehicles was offered, Enterprise also made "popular priced vehicles with a high standard." The carriages were shipped to all parts of the country as well as abroad, with a number going to Australia and India. The birth of the automobile, however, spelled the end of the carriage industry.

The plant started manufacturing an automobile, a roadster, which was completed, then destroyed in an accident. The brief automobile manufacturing operation ended, and Enterprise closed its doors in 1918. During World War I, the Wright Airplane Company took over the building and manufactured airplane parts there. (Courtesy of the Miamisburg Branch Library, Elmer Gaffney print.)

Jacob Kauffman, a woodworker from Pennsylvania, established the Kauffman Buggy Company (above) on Miami Avenue in 1869. His high-quality vehicles included phaetons, buggies, runabouts, surreys, road wagons, cabriolets, extension top carriages, victorias, and side-seat wagons. Daniel Bookwalter came to Miamisburg from neighboring Jefferson Township in 1849. After his original hub and spoke factory was absorbed by Kauffman Buggy, he moved to First Street and manufactured only wheels. At its peak in 1906, the Bookwalter Hub & Spoke factory (below) turned out as many as 35,000 sets of wheels a year and employed between 60 and 80 men a day. (Courtesy of the Miamisburg Historical Society, Image Industries prints.)

STAR CITY OPERA HOUSE, CHAS. BAUM, PROPR.

In addition to manufacturing operations, 1880s Miamisburg provided services including entertainment, lodging, and dining. Charles Baum was the proprietor of the Star City Opera House, also known as the Baum Opera House, located on First Street near the Miami and Erie Canal.

Washington House, the site of the Plaza Theater, had a longer history. When Miamisburg was incorporated as a village in 1832, the first election was held at the Jacob Wenger tavern, which later became the Washington House. The hotel's manager, Lorenz Wieland, was the great-grandfather of long-time Miami Township trustee Shirley Omietanski. (Courtesy of the Miamisburg Historical Society, Image Industries prints.)

Fred Beiswenger, a baker, came to Miamisburg from Germany (via Cincinnati) and opened his first market in 1869. He moved his bakery and confectionery business to "Beiswenger's Corner," on Market and Canal Streets in 1884. The candy counter was on the east side of the brick building; shelving on the west wall held loaves of bread; cases held gingersnaps and other baked goods; and the bakeshop was located in the rear. (Courtesy of the Miamisburg Historical Society, Image Industries print.)

Henry Groby, born in 1819, came to Miamisburg in 1838. Known as one of the best builders in the area, he also was interested in tobacco, real estate, farming, and lumber. With several partners, he formed H. Groby and Company in 1866 to "Receive deposits, discount commercial paper and sell exchange. Interest paid on time deposits." In 1888, the firm was granted a charter as the First National Bank of Miamisburg. (Courtesy of the Miamisburg Historical Society, Image Industries print.)

The Ohio Paper Company, organized in 1878, built its mill at the northern end of the city (near the Miami Valley Paper Company's mills) in 1879. Stockholders included John Weiser, Dr. T.V. Lyons, and his son T.V. Lyons, George Mays, and W.H. Albrecht. The company obtained its power from the Miamisburg Hydraulic Company. It was noted for its fine book and newsprint paper, but later turned to the manufacture of roofing paper. (Courtesy of the Miamisburg Historical Society, Image Industries print.)

The Miamisburg Binder Twine and Cordage Company, also known as the "Twine Factory," was organized in 1893. Its modern building, located near the southern end of the city on "Twine Mill Hill," east of the Miami and Erie Canal, was equipped with electricity and with automatic sprinklers for fire prevention. For years, Miamisburg residents could set their clocks by the "Twine Factory whistle." (Courtesy of the Miamisburg Historical Society, Image Industries print.)

Among the businesses located in the southeastern part of Miami Township east of Springboro Pike was that of Dr. R.B. Michel (Michet on an 1875 map). He owned land both north and south of today's Austin Road (probably including the site of Waldruhe Park). Dr. Michel's office was a small brick building located to the rear of his three-story brick home. He served as a physician in the 1800s and raised his own herbs for medicines. (Courtesy of Lee Hieronymus.)

"Waymer's Corners," once a township landmark, was located at the northwest corner of Miamisburg-Centerville Road and Springboro Pike. This painting by Bessie Griesmeyer depicts the Waymer service station and market as they looked in the 1950s. The artist and her family had a long association with the area: her grandfather managed the Washington House hotel in Miamisburg and her daughter served as a Miami Township trustee for 28 years. (Courtesy of Shirley Omietanski.)

George Friend came to Ohio in the 1860s from New York State. With his son, J. Howard Friend, he built a paper empire, beginning with the Friend Paper & Tablet Company, before 1900. The two assisted in the birth of all four West Carrollton paper mills—not actually building and operating them, but assisting with advice, money, land, and rental space to help the others get started.

In the beginning, their mill employed 70 of the town's 250 residents. Every family owed its living, directly or indirectly, to the mill. When the Friends' empire collapsed, around 1912, the new owners of Friend Paper changed the mill's name to the Miami Paper Company. (Courtesy of Dave Neuhardt.)

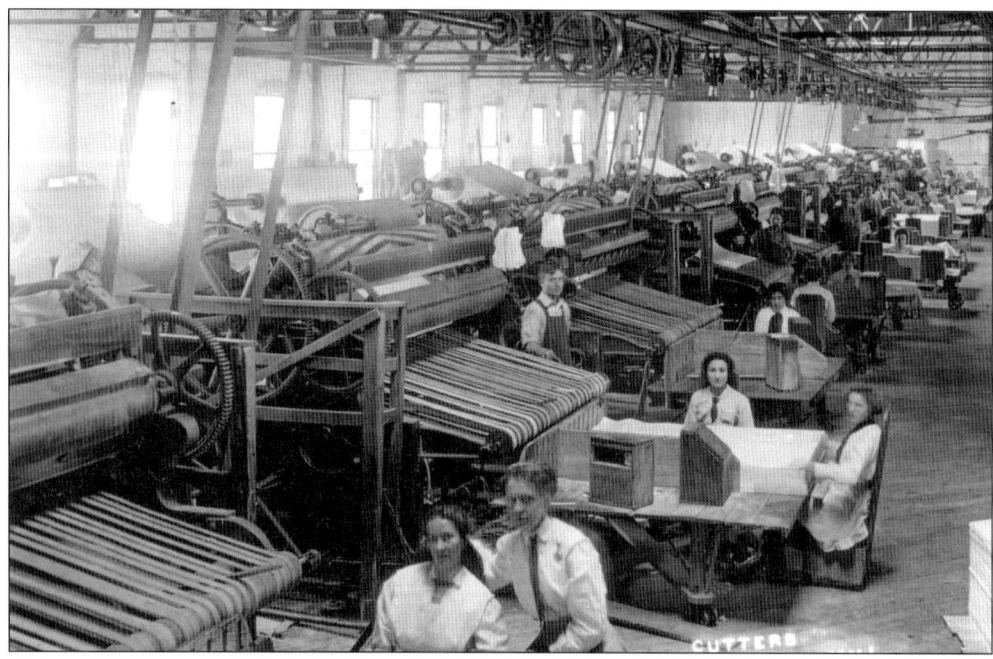

Once known as the "Paper City," West Carrollton was home to Friend Paper, Miami Paper, American Envelope, Karolton Envelope, Bergstrom Paper, and the West Carrollton Parchment Company. In 1899, Henry Newel came to Dayton from Massachusetts and, in a few rooms in the Parchment Company building, began making envelopes. He later joined with J. Howard Friend and Robert Burns in establishing the American Envelope Company. (Courtesy of Dave Neuhardt.)

In the 1890s, the Union Block building at the corner of Central Avenue and Elm Street in West Carrollton housed "Uncle Jim" Shannon's General Store on the ground floor. Sugar, rice, crackers, coffee, and mustard were sold in bulk; huge wheels of cheese were cut with a hand slicer. The building's third floor was a gathering place where basketball games were played and silent movies were shown (at which Goldie Throckmorton played the piano). (Courtesy of Dave Neuhardt.)

When Miamisburg celebrated its 150th anniversary in 1968, the city's leading industry, with nearly 2,000 workers, was the Monsanto Research Corporation's Mound Laboratory. It was located on a 180-acre site in the southern part of the city and was named for the nearby Miamisburg Mound, built by the prehistoric Native Americans known as the Adena Indians.

According to Mady Ransdell (in *Miamisburg: The Story of Our Town*), the laboratory's facilities were completed in 1948 and occupied in early 1949. The land, buildings, and equipment were owned by the U.S. Atomic Energy Commission, while the laboratory itself was operated by Monsanto Research Corporation (a subsidiary of Monsanto Corporation), under a contract with the AEC.

The first work at Mound Laboratory was in weapons parts, but the firm later became a production facility. Its work involved research, development, and production programs.

Less than 45 years after the facility opened, however, its closure was announced. Mound Lab had played a vital role in the city and the entire Miami Valley, but by 1992, it was no longer needed, and its work would move to other plants. The Department of Energy said the plant would shut down by 1996, although cleanup at the site would continue for a number of years.

The DOE also announced that part of $12 million in funding would be available to assist Miamisburg in finding new commercial uses for the 300-acre site on Mound Road. The funds were shared with two other communities also hit by the closure. (Courtesy of the Mound Museum Association.)

Seven
THE MIAMI VALLEY CHAUTAUQUA
1896–1946

In 1901, the Miami Valley Chautauqua, an institution formed in 1896 to provide popular education combined with entertainment in the form of lectures, concerts, and plays, moved into a site in Miami Township on the west bank of the Great Miami River, north of the Franklin Hydraulic Company's dam.

Over the years, speakers at the local Chautauqua included President William Howard Taft, Eleanor Roosevelt, evangelist Billy Sunday, and politician William Jennings Bryan. The country's best-known bands presented concerts on the club's enormous stage, and the summer program also included recreational activities, picnics, and an annual evening parade of lighted boats up and down the river.

According to Seymour Tibbals, one of the founders of the institution and the author of *Chautauqua Then and Now*, the Miami Valley Chautauqua (which no longer exists in its original form) was "a beautiful park along which flows a winding river…stately trees…a great lawn that reminds one of a well-kept college campus…picnic tables, outdoor ovens, refuse cans…a bell that breaks the stillness at times to call to worship or various conference sessions…a great stage upon which many men and women of fame have delivered messages to large audiences; trained birds, dogs and even an educated pig have appeared thereon; choruses, choirs, bands, orchestras and minstrels have sent forth music…a chapel in the woods that nestles beside the dam…a forum building in which earnest groups have studied and discussed many subjects from the doctrine of the atonement to the extermination of termites…a great dining hall where at times hundreds of hungry young people have been fed and an impatient diner growls because the service is too slow…a busy administration building where the general manager is beset with a thousand problems, where the mail is handled, telegrams filed, telephone messages relayed, cottages and cabins rented, reservations recorded, books kept, letters dictated—a veritable hive of industry…a drug store that handles the needs of its patrons from souvenir postcards to hot water bottles…a grocery that must supply food for the unexpected guest…a coffee shop that fries hamburgers by the thousands…a tiny tots' playground with swinging ponies, slides and teeters…a miniature golf course that has revived a sport that was once as dead as a door nail…vast tennis courts, a model swimming pool, bowling alleys, roller skating rink and boats and bicycles for hire…a lodging house, the Frances Willard cottage for women, cabins, trailers and cottages…great crowds of people and parked automobiles, baseball games and supervised contests upon occasion…family reunions in the shelter houses, industrial picnics that come in chartered buses…high school bands…cottage house parties and families who make their permanent home here…babies, children, adolescent youth, puppy love, dates and the holding of hands…through the mystical whirl, under the pale moon, walking along the river's banks, the old, but ever new experience of boy meets girl.

"Today," he wrote in 1946, "the grandchildren of couples who first met at Miami Valley Chautauqua are coming to splash in the kiddies' wading pool. No wonder so many people love Chautauqua. It is so fragrant with fond memories, so filled with the scenes and joys of bygone days that are pushed back into the shadows by the romping, laughing, singing horde of youngsters who fill the place in the good old summer time."

The local Chautauqua movement began in July 1896 when the Reverend Thomas Harrison from Massachusetts led a revival service at the old Franklin fairgrounds. The 11-day camp meeting included evangelistic services each evening. The daily program began with a sunrise prayer meeting, followed by religious services. Two of the speakers on "G.A.R. Day," however, gave addresses that stood out from the sermons—and caused the camp meeting to be changed to the Miami Valley Chautauqua the next summer.

The man referred to as the "real father of Chautauqua" was the Reverend E.A. Harper, a Methodist minister in Germantown. He was quick to sense the keen interest in seeing and hearing men of wide reputation outside the realm of the church. As a result, the religious camp meeting was changed to the broader Chautauqua format.

The first real Miami Valley Chautauqua assembly was launched in 1897. It began with a five-day religious camp meeting held at the fairgrounds. Many notable speakers appeared that year; sermons were preached, but there were also lectures, including one with music. The only complaint from the local farmers was that the cost of attending the assembly was too high.

In 1898, F. Gillum Cromer, the president of the Miami Valley Chautauqua Company, said: "The summer assembly has solved the problem of happily uniting recreation and profit, and filling a vacation with intellectual and spiritual uplift." Tents were provided for campers that year, and the stalls in the old fairgrounds were used as sleeping quarters. A dining room was set up in the Art Hall, and the auditorium was a big circus tent. The assembly was limited to nine days, covering two weekends.

Assemblies continued at the Franklin fairgrounds in 1899 and 1900. In 1899, William Jennings Bryan made his first appearance at the Miami Valley Chautauqua and brought widespread fame and popularity to the institution. The fifth, and last, assembly held at the fairgrounds was in August 1900. Before the advertising materials were sent out, 200 tents had

PANARAMA VIEW OF MIAMI VALLEY CHAUTAUQUA.

been engaged for the Chautauqua camp, and all the horse stalls were rented. That year's program marked the first deviation from the previous schedule of sermons, lectures, and music: a French illusionist and prestidigitator appeared in an "entertainment of mystery and mirth."

Forty years later, it was evident that the public's interest in assemblies was waning as the scope of Chautauqua's other activities had broadened. An effort was made to revive interest in the assembly program in the early 1940s. A plan was adopted to reduce the assembly period to nine evening attractions, with the addition of three Sunday afternoon lectures by noteworthy talent. One of those lectures was delivered by Eleanor Roosevelt.

Early in 1941, Chautauqua management entered into a cooperative agreement with Cincinnati radio station WLW to broadcast seven Sunday afternoon programs directly from Chautauqua. On Sunday, June 29, the "Quiz Kids," a nationally known program, opened the series of broadcasts. In July, H.V. Kaltenborn, a well-known commentator over the NBC-Red Network, gave his nationwide broadcast from the Miami Valley Chautauqua.

In 1942, with America's involvement in World War II, it was recommended that swimming pools, skating rinks, and other places of amusement be kept going at full speed, and that forum meetings, platform discussions, and lectures be conducted wherever possible. Then government restrictions were imposed. The assembly program was completely abandoned because of gasoline rationing and wartime restrictions on travel.

As the war neared its end, management of the debt-plagued program was turned over to the cottage owners, who made up the newly formed Miami Valley Chautauqua Association. Sixty years later, the Chautauqua community remains a part of Miami Township, while the Chautauqua grounds are rented by a church group. (Courtesy of the Franklin Historical Society and of Sue and Bruce Walker.)

In the early 1900s, traction (electric railway) cars brought visitors to Chautauqua's river bridge entrance. This entrance was destroyed when the Great Miami River overflowed its banks during the 1913 Flood. The following year a pontoon bridge was laid across the river just below the dam. The distance from the traction car stop to the auditorium was about the same as before the flood—and people continued to attend summer programs. (Courtesy of Mark Renwick.)

The year 1901 marked the first season for Chautauqua at its new site in Miami Township, just north of the Franklin Hydraulic Company's dam. The move from the Franklin fairgrounds gave the Miami Valley Chautauqua a permanent home for its annual assemblies. A large auditorium, a dining hall (later destroyed by fire), and other buildings were ready for use on Chautauqua's opening day: Friday, July 26, 1901. (Courtesy of the Franklin Historical Society.)

Visitors to Chautauqua commented on its shaded streets and the pride taken in its cottages. The roads were kept in good condition, and the summer houses were well-maintained.

When Eleanor Roosevelt came to make a speech in 1940, she wrote about her visit in her newspaper column, "My Day": "We drove to Chautauqua, Ohio, straight from the train and as we entered this widely-known summer resort we passed gay parties and boats on the Miami River. The big swimming pool and tennis courts were crowded with young people. The cottages looked unpretentious, but attractive and comfortable. The place impressed me as being thoroughly American and an ideal spot for a vacation."

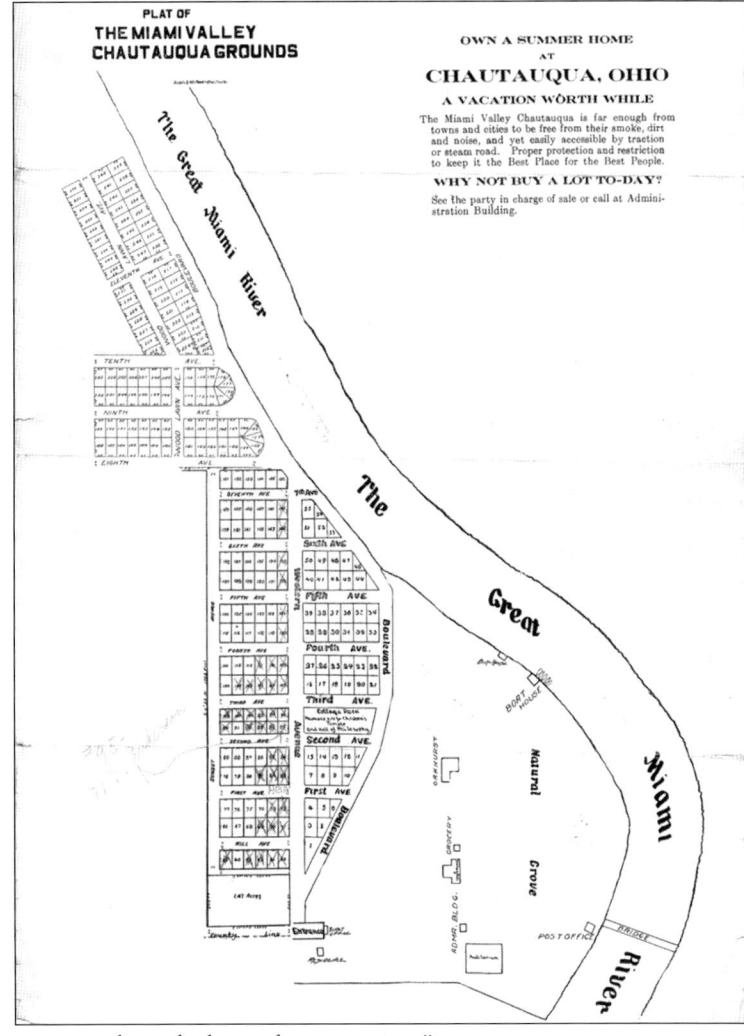

And it was. One of the reasons the local Chautauqua was established was to enhance family life and provide a wholesome place for children and young people to play.

When the Miami Valley Chautauqua outgrew its Franklin fairgrounds location and began looking around for another site, one of the two proposed locations was the Van Derveer Grove in neighboring Miami Township. The township location was chosen, and its first season (1901) was a success. The tent city of summer visitors continued to grow, necessitating the purchase of 40 more acres of land in 1902.

Lots were surveyed and offered for sale to those who wished to build cottages. By 1904, 16 cottages had been built—and the white "city of tents" reached its peak. Four years later, there were 60 private cottages. Lot purchasers were given warranty deeds with restrictions that would prevent Chautauqua from ever being other than a desirable place for summer homes. The grounds were the only location in Ohio that were bought, owned, and operated solely for Chautauqua purposes.

Growth was steady. In 1909, Chautauqua was recognized by the U.S. Post Office Department, which granted a new summer post office—putting Chautauqua on the map and greatly pleasing the growing colony of summer residents. (Courtesy of the Franklin Historical Society.)

Between 1928 and 1937, Chautauquans saw 18 cabins built on Cabin Row, along with two shelter houses and a new dining hall. One reason for the growth was a sewer and water project, initiated in 1935 through the government's WPA program, that brought running water from the Franklin Water Works system to Chautauqua. Property values also increased when the sanitary sewer system was introduced, and flush toilets were installed. (Courtesy of the Franklin Historical Society.)

In the mid-1930s, people began spending more time at Chautauqua and improving their cottages. Instead of an 18-day occupation (as in former years), practically all of the cottages were occupied during the entire summer season. By the mid-1940s, most cottages had been winterized for year-round living. Property values had increased, and new families were purchasing cottages for their own use rather than as summer rental units. (Courtesy of Julia Shupert Hagwood.)

As support for the old-time assembly programs began to decrease, and it became more difficult to find nationally known attractions at an affordable price, greater effort was made to attract conventions, conferences, and reunions to Chautauqua. The old Grandview Hotel (above) was renovated and made more comfortable. Roads and streets were repaired. Up-to-date recreational features were planned and built. From the beginning, however, the Miami Valley Chautauqua was often on the verge of bankruptcy. The Board of Managers and the business office (below) found that, despite assessments, lodging, and concession fees, they couldn't always make a profit—or break even. (Courtesy of the Franklin Historical Society.)

In 1927, a decision was made to offer free admission to the grounds. The plan to make Chautauqua more of a summer resort with interesting features running from Decoration (Memorial) Day to Labor Day met with immediate public approval. Attendance throughout the season was larger than it had been for several years. Between 1928 and 1937, a number of new features were built on the grounds, including an up-to-date swimming pool. Young people flocked to the beach and the pool, and enjoyed the new bowling alleys and nighttime roller-skating on the tennis courts. (Courtesy of the Franklin Historical Society.)

When the Miami Valley Chautauqua first moved to the site in Miami Township, a three-span iron footbridge was erected over the river. Twelve hundred trees of 40 varieties were transplanted, adding to the beauty of the grounds. Years later, cottagers and visitors alike appreciated the shady areas around the park, the cabins, and the cottage sections. (Courtesy of the Franklin Historical Society.)

The Great Miami River, broad and majestic along the two-mile-long stretch of Chautauqua frontage, formed a curve on the north, then bent to the east. It was a perfect place to go canoeing. (Courtesy of the Franklin Historical Society.)

The 1930s saw the construction of two shuffleboard courts. They proved so popular that three additional courts were installed in the 1940s. Other improvements included five cement tennis courts (and the resurfacing of the cottagers' private tennis courts) and a baseball diamond. A stable was built and riding horses were brought to Chautauqua because it was thought that horseback riding would prove popular with the young people. The year 1940 also marked the return of "Tom Thumb" golf, when a concession was granted for a miniature golf course at the Coffee Shop corner near the end of Main Street. (Courtesy of the Franklin Historical Society.)

From its earliest days, the Miami Valley Chautauqua's stated purpose was to provide a wholesome place where young people could meet and play. It was a place to be enjoyed by family members of every age. In 2004, adults still reminisce about how much fun they had as children, taking a ride around the grounds on the little train. Additional activities for younger children included a "boat race" ride and other concessions—and there was always the playground, with its swings, slides, and teeter-totters. For older children, there were bicycles and boats to rent. (Courtesy of the Franklin Historical Society.)

The most damaging of all the spring floods to affect Chautauqua took place in March 1913. The Great Flood tore through the park and reached to the foundations of the Grandview Hotel. Cottages and buildings on the lower level were swept away, the bridge across the river was gone, and the grove of trees was ruined. No assembly program could be held that summer. Chautauqua was devastated; the entire Miami Valley was digging out of the mud, and no one gave any thought to vacations. Later floods, like those that inundated Skateland's parking lot (above) and cottage lawns (below), were minor by comparison. (Courtesy of the Franklin Historical Society.)

Eight
First Churches and Schools
1803–1927

Throughout the 1800s, the pioneers came, by foot and by river, to the area that would become Miami Township. Early settlers, with the exception of a few families from Virginia and North Carolina, were mostly from eastern Pennsylvania. Their language was the Pennsylvania Dutch dialect, and their church affiliation was either Lutheran or German Reformed.

Hand in hand with the early settlements came the first churches and schoolhouses. The earliest schools in the northern area of the township were in Alexanderville (1817) and Carrollton (a two-room log building erected in 1825). The first schools in the Miamisburg area were at Gebhart (St. John's) Meeting House and Stettler Church (both prior to 1818) and Jacob's Schoolhouse (1818). They were maintained mostly by German Reformed and Lutheran congregations and took on the nature of parochial schools.

The church has always figured prominently in the history of a community. In Miamisburg, there are five churches whose roots go deep into the history of the city. The northern part of the township was home to several other early churches.

The first religious services in the Miamisburg area were conducted in Zachariah Hole's stockade by Reverend John Kobler, a Methodist missionary sent to the area about 1797. He recorded in his diary that on August 13, 1798, he rode down the big Miami 12 miles and preached in an old fortress to a small congregation of a few families who lived in the fort (Hole's Station).

Among the earliest congregations in Miamisburg were Stettler Lutheran Church, Gebhart (St. John) Lutheran Church, the German Reformed Church (today's Trinity United Church of Christ), St. Jacob's Lutheran Church, and St. Michael's Chapel (Our Lady of Good Hope Church).

In the Carrollton area, the first churches were Memorial Methodist, First Presbyterian, and Grace Lutheran. In the northeastern part of what would become the township, there was Zion Church, which later became today's Zion Memorial United Church of Christ (now located in Moraine), and Zion Evangelical Lutheran Church.

The first schools were very basic. According to Jacob Zimmer, writing in *Beer's History of Montgomery County* in 1882: "The early educational facilities here, as elsewhere in frontier life, were very ordinary."

In the *Montgomery County History and Annual* (1926), Miamisburg educator Harris Bear said that very little is known of the early history of Miami Township's schools. He added that the first log schoolhouses in the area were probably built at Alexanderville (today's West Carrollton) and just east of Miamisburg (the St. John's/Gebhart schoolhouse).

A law initiating Ohio's public school system was passed in 1852. After the law was enacted, Jacob Zimmer wrote that "(T)he Township Board of Education…commenced to build new (school)houses in nearly every district. The log cabin schoolhouse was abandoned, while new and comfortable quarters, with modern improved seats and desks, took the place of slab seats and log fires."

By the early 1900s, there were four public elementary schools located in Miami Township. The two northern schools became part of the West Carrollton Village School District in 1924, while the two southern schools became part of the newly created Miamisburg Village School District in 1926.

Stettler Church, the oldest Lutheran church in Ohio, was established in 1803 on South Union Road west of the Great Miami River. Several families, including the Shuperts, the Stettlers, and the Gebharts, bought land at $6.50 an acre, cleared away the woods between the river and Twin Creek, planted crops, and established a church on land that was given by the Stettler family. Known as the "ridge" church because of its location on a hill, the church flourished for many years, but merged with St. John's (Gebhart) Lutheran Church in 1976. Stettler Church was torn down in the early 21st century, but the old cemetery remains. Many familiar names appear on the headstones, including Stettler, Pontius, Hoffman, Libecap, Kuhn, Gebhart, Focht, and Shupert. (Courtesy of Julia Shupert Hagwood.)

Reverend Jacob LaRose established a congregation of Lutheran and German Reformed settlers who built the Society of St. John's Meeting House in 1805. The two-room log structure was the first church in Washington Township (from which Miami Township was formed). Church services were held in one room, school classes in the other. A new church, built in 1818, was also known as Gebhart Church because the George Gebhart family sold the land to the congregation for $10. (Courtesy of Lee Hieronymus.)

The first official burial in St. John's cemetery was in 1806 for Christine Baum, born in 1762. Unofficially (based on a scrap of paper found in the church's archives), the first person buried at the cemetery was a freed slave, a companion and farmhand who came to the area from North Carolina in 1804 with the Gebhart family. The deed for the two-acre property at the corner of Gebhart Church and Maue roads was recorded in 1816. (Courtesy of Paul Tucker.)

The Reverend John Casper Dill organized the Evangelical Lutheran congregation of Jacob's Schoolhouse in 1821 and oversaw the union with the Reformed congregation. Five years later, Pastor Henry Heincke (whose sermons were delivered in German) took charge of the congregation. While still worshipping in the schoolhouse, members began building a $3,200 brick church. The cornerstone of Jacob's Church was laid in 1830, and the church was dedicated in 1833. (Picture from the *Combination Atlas Map of Montgomery County*.)

Another early Miamisburg church was the German Reformed congregation, organized in 1820, which joined in maintaining and worshipping at Jacob's Schoolhouse. The Reformed congregation decided to erect a church of their own in 1860, so joint occupancy of Jacob's Church was dissolved. The First Reformed Church (today's Trinity United Church of Christ) at the corner of Second and Linden was completed in 1861 and dedicated in 1863. A large brick church was constructed in 1900. (Courtesy of Trinity United Church of Christ.)

In 1845, a Methodist Sunday School began meeting in the homes of various Carrollton-area residents. The next year, Perry Pease offered a site on North Locust Street and started subscriptions to build a Methodist Episcopal Meeting House (today's Memorial United Methodist Church). The building was completed in 1848 and refurbished in 1885. Then the "May cyclone" blew the roof off, depositing it on Central Avenue. A larger stone church was built in 1906. (Courtesy of the West Carrollton Historical Society.)

The church of the First Presbyterian Society of Carrollton (at left) was built on the corner of Main and Walnut streets in 1846. The land was deeded to the church by Horace Pease. Grace Evangelical Lutheran Church (at right) held its first services in 1865 when five farm families in the Carrollton area organized their own congregation. An abandoned schoolhouse on Walnut Street was purchased in 1876, and the first communion service was held in 1878. (Courtesy of Dave Neuhardt.)

From 1820 to 1843, a log cabin served as the first church for a 12-member congregation called the Zion Society. They united with the German Evangelical Lutheran Church and held worship services in the home of Peter Hetzel at the corner of Dogwood Lane and Stroop Road in the northeastern part of what would become Miami Township. The first ministers who served Zion were circuit riders. (Courtesy of Zion Evangelical Lutheran Church.)

The two-story brick Zion Church (today's Zion Memorial United Church of Christ) on South Dixie Drive cost about $3,500 to build. The congregation completed construction in 1857 and dedicated the new structure in 1860. In May 1886, a cyclone partially destroyed the church, tearing away the steeple and part of the east wall of the church building. The church was repaired, but the union dissolved when the Lutheran part of the congregation decided to build separately. (Courtesy of Zion Memorial United Church of Christ.)

Zion Evangelical Lutheran Church, built at a cost of $5,000 on an acre of ground from the John Emert farm, was dedicated in 1887. The congregation remained at that location for more than 70 years before purchasing four acres of land on Munger Road in 1959. The last service in the old church was held in May 1960, with the first worship service and Sunday school in the new buildings held a year later, in June 1961. (Courtesy of Zion Evangelical Lutheran Church.)

In 1852, Michael Cassilly of Cincinnati donated a two-story brick house on Lock Street for a Catholic church. St. Michael's Chapel was on the second floor, with living quarters for a future pastor on the first floor. The Reverend Henry Damian Yunker (or Junker) celebrated the first Mass. A new church was dedicated in July 1881 as "Our Immaculate Lady of Good Hope." Today's church, dedicated in 1971, is on Central Avenue at South Third Street. (Courtesy of the Miamisburg Historical Society, Image Industries print.)

A Township

6	5	4	3	2	1
7	8	9	10	11	12
18	17	**16**	15	14	13
19	20	21	22	23	24
30	29	28	27	26	25
31	32	33	34	35	36

*Congress reserved **section 16** near the middle of each township for the use of public schools.*

According to *The Official Ohio Lands Book*, the U.S. government granted more than 704,000 acres of public (federal) land to the state of Ohio for the support of public schooling.

Each of the state's townships received Section 16 whenever possible, or another section in lieu of it. Early land grants sometimes meant that Section 16 was not available, so it was not uncommon for a substitute section to be assigned.

In April 1803, Ohio's first state legislature provided for the leasing and administering of school lands. Initially, the lands were to be leased for seven to fifteen years. The lessee had to clear and fence the property, plant 100 apple trees, and perform other duties.

Later, some legislators wanted to sell school lands. In 1826, Congress permitted sales with the provision that the township's residents must vote their consent. The voting, appraisal, and conveyance procedures to be followed were enacted in January 1827. Proceeds from the sale of school lands were deposited in the Common School fund, and interest on the principal was paid to the schools within the original surveyed township.

At one time, Miami Township had 13 school districts or sub-districts (including Chautauqua, as well as a partial district shared with Jefferson Township). The township schools were "rural" schools, for students in grades one through eight. Although Miami Township had a high school for a short time, most students of high school age attended schools in the Miamisburg and West Carrollton school districts. (Map from *The Official Ohio Lands Book*.)

This early schoolhouse also served as a place of worship until 1833. When the first half of the Miamisburg settlement was laid out (platted) and offered for sale in 1818, the community felt it was of great importance that a school be established.

By July of that year, a frame (or log) schoolhouse was built on what is now the corner of Central Avenue and First Street. After a few years, the school was moved eastward to make room for construction of the Miami and Erie Canal. The building still stands today and is located on South Second Street near Central Avenue.

In *Miamisburg: The Story of Our Town*, Esther Light wrote that articles of agreement as to the building's use were drawn up by the Reverend William Dechant, who was said to have organized the German Reformed congregations at Stettler Church (west of the river on Union Road) and St. John's, located on Gebhart Church Road. The agreement covered more than education: it contained instructions for public worship, funerals, and other meetings of public interest.

Since the school was maintained mostly by the German Reformed and the Lutheran congregations, it was similar to a parochial school. (Courtesy of Trinity United Church of Christ.)

Nellie Swartzel (at left), the teacher at Miami Township School Number 9, joined her students for a group picture in 1908. A picture of a newer schoolhouse, also Number 9, shows that the school was built in 1911. Robert Jones (fifth from the left) sits on the stoop. A few years later a Montgomery County "model school," an initiative to improve schools and inspire teachers in Miami and other townships, was located at this schoolhouse. (Courtesy of Jim and Diane Woolf.)

Miami Township School Number 4 was located on State Route 741 (Springboro Pike) on land donated by Jonathan Gebhart. The group photograph, taken in 1912, shows Miss Alice Hetzler, the one-room school's teacher, and students, including young Harriet Gebhart (fourth from left), who is also pictured outside the school. After the school closed in 1926, the building was purchased by the Fellowship Baptist Church. (Courtesy of Lee Hieronymus.)

Posing for this school photograph, taken in 1890, were the students who attended the Carrollton public school. At that time, all grades were taught in one building. The Baker twins were seated in the second row at the right. Maggie Eicher, wearing a white apron, stood at the left, and Pearl Shock stood in the back row, second from left. (Courtesy of the West Carrollton Historical Society.)

The villages of Carrollton and Alexanderville formed a single school district, and in 1876, built what was called at the time a "fine (school)house halfway between the towns. The educational facilities being all that could be desired"—at least by 1880s standards. The four-room brick schoolhouse was located on the site of today's Middle School on Central Avenue. In 1893, the school was expanded when two rooms were added to the building. (Courtesy of Dave Neuhardt.)

A two-year high school course was added to the curriculum at the "union" schoolhouse in 1894, and six students graduated in 1896. In 1909, the high school course was increased to four years. The first graduation from the West Carrollton High School building took place in 1914. Mr. J.H. Bouts was pictured, standing in the top row at the right. Also in the top row were Irvin Ray (second from left) and Elbert Edmonson (fourth from left). Bob McNabb was seated at the right end of the third row. The composite picture from the "Piratan" yearbook (below) shows the school's growth through the 1900s. (Courtesy of the West Carrollton Historical Society.)

One of Miamisburg's oldest elementary schools is Kinder (Auditorium) School, built on East Central Avenue in 1906. In 1926, educator Harris Bear said: "Miamisburg schools emphasize the fundamental and traditional subjects, such as reading, arithmetic, spelling, geography, history. (F)rom the fifth grade up, a definite scheme of visitation to the industrial plants of the community makes for more intelligent study of the possibilities open to each child in the selection of a future career." (Courtesy of *The Miamisburg/West Carrollton News*.)

Members of the Stump family attended one of the local "country" schools. Pictured in this undated school photograph are three family members, along with their classmates and teacher. William Stump is seated in the first row, to the right of his teacher. Standing in the back row are D.A. Stump (fifth from left) and Cora Stump (sixth from left). (Courtesy of the Miamisburg Board of Education.)

Wantz School, named for long-time Miamisburg educator Anna K. Wantz, was built in 1927 and attended by "intermediate" students in grades six through eight. It was one of several buildings erected on land acquired in the mid-1800s for schools. When the present high school opened in 1972, some realignment took place in the district's other schools. Today, the Wantz building houses only seventh and eighth grade students. (Courtesy of *The Miamisburg/West Carrollton News*.)

In this undated picture, two of the Stump children, Alma and Paul, were photographed in front of Wantz Intermediate School on a snowy winter day. (Courtesy of the Miamisburg Board of Education.)

As the number of Miamisburg children grew, the village voted a tax of $2,500 to build a schoolhouse on a half-acre site purchased from the corporation cemetery on East Central Avenue (the site of today's Library Park). A two-story brick building located on Central Avenue just west of the railroad tracks opened in 1850. A second wing was added at the rear of the school in 1868.

A high school department was started at the school, and the first class graduated in 1873. Eventually, the two-wing schoolhouse was overflowing, so three two-story frame buildings were added to the school grounds. In 1891, the red brick building known as the "arch schoolhouse" was erected on the Central Avenue site, next to the high school (the present site of Our Lady of Good Hope Church). The arch building was followed by Kercher Street School (1899), Kinder School (1906), the South High School (1922), Wantz School (1927), and the North High School (1963).

When the Board of Education determined that some of the oldest school buildings were no longer needed, much of the site on Central Avenue with buildings was sold in 1923. By the 1960s, plans were made to build a new high school in order to free up the North High School building (today's Neff School) to house other grades. In 1968, the school district acquired a 61-acre site at the corner of Gebhart Church and Belvo Roads. Constructed in pods, with open-space interior design, it originally housed students in grades 10 through 12. Freshman moved into the building after a reorganization.

The South High School (pictured above), later known as the Maude Bell building, was torn down in the 1980s. (Courtesy of Lee Hieronymus.)

Nine
HISTORIC EVENTS
1800s–1988

Those who live in the valley of the Great Miami River have experienced a number of historic events. Some, like the visits of President Theodore Roosevelt to Miamisburg and the visit of Vice President George Bush to West Carrollton, are remembered with pleasure. Others brought neighbors together just to survive: floods and epidemics, tornadoes and cyclones, blizzards and train derailments.

In *Miamisburg: The Story of Our Town*, Esther Light told a story she'd heard about an early flood in which the Great Miami River spanned the valley from hill to hill. It might have taken place during the Great Flood of 1805, she said, which (according to Montgomery County history) occurred after pouring rains continued for nearly a week, and the Miami River rose and completely filled its channel.

An 1852 Miamisburg church record indicated that an epidemic of "flux" (or dysentery) had spread through the area. Before it ended, 21 infants and some adults had died from the disease. Another epidemic had occurred several years earlier. One of the victims was Dr. Silas Smith, a surgeon. In 1864, Dr. Isaac Reiter, a minister at what would become Miamisburg's Trinity Church, reported on a disease he thought was "flu" or dysentery, with many fatal cases. He conducted 14 funerals in 16 days—and attended 47 funerals for the year. That was a heavy schedule for a small congregation, as 30 of the deceased were members of the church.

Local newspapers reported that a tornado struck the area between five and six in the evening on June 9, 1860, "heralded by a hoarse rumbling similar to a train of cars." The storm lifted Miamisburg's Linden Avenue bridge from its masonry and hurled it, in ruins, into the river bed. It swept across the town, tearing the roofs off houses, destroying chimneys, and uprooting trees. Jacob Zimmer, who lived west of the river, described the tornado this way: "Cows, horses and pigs were unceremoniously hustled along or lifted from their feet, and rolled about in the most undignified manner; and ducks, geese, chickens and other fowls shot through the air with a velocity rarely witnessed."

A cyclone swept through in May 1886, shortly after the Methodist Church in West Carrollton had been refurbished. The May cyclone blew the entire roof off the church, depositing it on Central Avenue. The congregation decided that the Lord didn't like the old flat roof, so they replaced it with one that was much steeper. The same cyclone partially destroyed Zion Church in Miami Township, tearing away the steeple and the east wall of the church building. That congregation also rebuilt after the storm, including the steeple.

Late winter and early spring rains brought more flooding to the area in 1898 and again in the early 1900s. But the Great Flood of 1913 is the one that the communities along the river will never forget. Much of Chautauqua, Miamisburg, and West Carrollton were under water. In Miamisburg, the river rose to 11 feet on Main Street, and almost all of West Carrollton's downtown area was inundated. Bridges and houses were swept away. No future flood would ever compare with the devastation caused by the one in 1913.

More recently, there was the blizzard of 1978, a late January storm that shut down schools, businesses, and most government services, and a 1986 train derailment and phosphorus fire with dangerous fumes that forced 30,000 area residents from their homes for 93 hours. If not significantly historic, these were at least memorable events.

When President Theodore Roosevelt visited Miamisburg in the early 1900s, he spoke to the crowds from the Miamisburg Twine and Cordage Company located on "Twine Mill Hill." (Courtesy of the Miamisburg Historical Society.)

When the Great Miami River overflowed its banks in March 1898, the event was captured in this photograph. Spring flooding was common along the river. The town of Bridgeport (at the west end of Miamisburg's Linden Avenue bridge) was usually inundated, and it wasn't unusual for Miami Avenue (on the east side of the river) to be flooded too. (Courtesy of *The Miamisburg/West Carrollton News*.)

Another postcard depicting the March 1898 flood showed the rising waters threatening the base of a covered bridge—and Miamisburg residents looking for signs the floodwaters were beginning to recede. (Courtesy of Dave Neuhardt.)

Before the Great Flood in 1913, there had been rain for several days—so much rain, in fact, that it broke all records for this part of the country. On the morning of March 25, those living along the river awoke to see it overflowing its banks. The water kept rising throughout the day, forcing those living nearest the river to evacuate their homes. By the next day, this was the scene on Miamisburg's Third Street looking north. (Courtesy of Esther Light.).

This was the scene from Cedar Hill in south Miamisburg looking down at the Waterworks, where floodwater had entered the dynamo room of the water and light plant about noon on March 25. The flood marooned many families on the second floors of their homes or on the upper floors of business buildings on Main Street. The streets closest to the river were filled with debris, including sheds, stables, and wrecked homes. Both river bridges were gone. (Courtesy of the Miamisburg Historical Society.)

The footbridge entrance to Chautauqua where passengers disembarked from the traction cars was swept away by the flood. The old bridge could not be replaced, so a pontoon bridge was laid across the river (just below the dam) before the next summer assembly opened.

When the floodwaters subsided, they left behind mounds of debris. In Miamisburg, the flood residue included jackknifed traction cars on Main Street and tilted telephone poles on First Street. Four days after the flood, the water and lights were back on. Gas service was restored in a week. (Courtesy of Dave Neuhardt.)

In January 1978, a 14-inch snowfall closed area schools. Later that month, on January 26, rain poured down on the area, followed by a sharp drop in temperature. Then came wind gusts of more then 70 miles an hour—plus an additional five or six inches of snow. During the 1978 blizzard, everything stopped. Schools and businesses closed. Cars were towed; a frozen engine kept a helicopter grounded at the Moraine Airpark. Snow plows and crews worked double shifts, and those who owned snowmobiles delivered milk, groceries, and medicine. After the cleanup, snow was piled high along streets in the Sherwood Forest neighborhood (below) and throughout the township. (Courtesy of the Dayton Daily News, photographs by Richard Anderson and Charlie Steinbrunner.)

The great train derailment and fire took place on July 7, 1986. A 44-car freight train derailed on the B&O (today's CSX) tracks west of the river in Miamisburg, losing its last four cars and their cargo. When oxygen came in contact with the 20,000 gallons of white phosphorous in a tanker, fire and smoke erupted. Flames leaped 60 to 70 feet in the air. A state of emergency was declared; thousands of people were forced from their homes for four days. (Courtesy of *The Miamisburg/West Carrollton News*.)

After the train derailment, as clouds of dangerous white smoke filled the sky, many people were evacuated to the Dayton Mall—then evacuated again when the Mall itself had to be closed. Later in July, the assistant manager of the Mall (at left) presented Miami Township Fire Chief B.K. Ring with a plaque and a note of thanks for his assistance during the emergency and for the aid provided by members of the Fire Department.

West Carrollton's annual Paper Festival hosted some special visitors on August 20,1988: Vice President George Bush and his wife Barbara, and Bush's running mate, Dan Quayle and his wife Marilyn. After they walked the flag-lined parade route on Saturday morning, the Republican candidate for president spoke at a rally in Weidner Park (the former site of the Miami and Erie Canal). At the park's T-ball diamond, scouts flanked the stage lined by local dignitaries under a banner that read, "Welcome to our hometown." Bush began his Ohio campaign for the presidency by giving his "Heartland" speech: "I'm glad to be in the heartland," he said. "You can feel the patriotism in this part of the country." (Courtesy of *The Miamisburg/West Carrollton News* and Carrollton Hills Girl Scout Neighborhood.)

Ten
TOWNSHIP GOVERNMENT—
SERVICE FIRST
1829–2004

"Township government—service first": These words are a reminder to elected officials, department heads and staff, as well as to those who live and work in the township, of Miami Township's 175-year history of service.

A complete list of those who have guided the township over the past 175 years is not available, as election records for the first 80 years of the township's existence have proved difficult to locate. Early records show that on April 5, 1830, in Miami Township's first election, voters chose three trustees: John Neibel, Fletcher Emly, and Benjamin Sayre; a clerk, Thomas Morton; and a treasurer, Charles Connelly.

According to the *Journal of the Proceedings of the Trustees* (dated 1837), those serving as trustees in April 1836 were Henry Gephart, John Neibel, and Jacob Eagle. In November, the journal also listed Thomas Dodds as a trustee. The clerk was John Conley; Peter Reichard was the treasurer.

In April 1837, the trustees were Henry Gephart, James Morton, and Jacob Eagle. John Conley was clerk and Peter Reichard was treasurer. In an election held on April 1, 1839, Eagle and Gephart were reelected, and William Brooks was elected trustee. John Conley was reelected clerk, and David Hoover was elected treasurer.

Election results for 1873, published in the *Miamisburg Bulletin*, list those elected to the position of trustee: T. White, J.W. Hipple, and John Mayer (or Moyer), who tied with another candidate and won with a coin toss. Elected to the clerk's position was J.A. Schuster; S.H. Hager was elected treasurer.

A more recent listing of those who have served as trustee or clerk-treasurer begins in the 20th century: John Eicher, John Storck and William Cade (1909–1911); George Schmidt (1912–1921); Frank Eagle (1912–1913); Isaac Zehring (1912–1933); Sam Studybaker (1914–1915, 1924–1933); John Storck (1916–1921); Simon Recher (1924–1933); Howard (C.H.) Bloss (1936–1953); George Leis (1936–1965); Charles Leisz (1936–1941); Walter Byers (1946–1955); James Good (1954–1963); Edmund Rice (1956–1963); William McCabe (1964–1975); Byron Grooms (1964–1969); Oscar Page (1966–1977); Ray Wolfe (1972–1975); James Cogan (1976–1977); Shirley Omietanski (1976–2003); Berman Layer (1978–1997); Douglas Zink (1978–1981, 1994–); Ron Hall (1982–1985); Patrick Meyer (1986–1989); David Coffey (1998–); and Charles Lewis (2004–).

Those serving as the township's clerk-treasurer during the same period included: John Peiffer (1909–1911); Charles Eicher (1912–1921); F. Edwin Treon (1924–1933); H.W. Albrecht (1936–1939); Paul Rice (1940–1967); Gerald Malott (1968–1977); Frank Cleary (1978–1997); Kimberly Banford (1997); and Deborah Preston (1998–2004).

In recent years, an administrator has been hired to run the day-to-day operation of the township: David Anderson (1995–2002); Police Chief John "Chris" Krug (acting administrator, 2002); and Gregory Hanahan (2002–2004).

Also carrying out Miami Township's long tradition of service are the members of the Fire Department, Planning and Zoning Department, Police Department and Service Department, the Park Board, and other boards and commissions, and all those involved in township administration, including finance and human resources. They all know the importance of providing "service first" to township residents and businesses.

In the 1970s, when this picture was taken, the Police Department had not yet moved into its new headquarters at 2660 Lyons Road. At that time, only three men had served as chief of police: Albert Engle, Estis Lawrence, and Edward (Woody) Woodward. Chief Woodward (kneeling, third from left) served the township from 1963 to 1978, during the time the Dayton Mall was built, when many police officers were volunteers.

The Police Department is made up of four divisions: police, records, dispatch, and administration. The mission of every member of the department is to provide assistance to those who cannot care for themselves, to protect the innocent, and to bring offenders to justice. Filling out accident reports (pictured here) is only one of their many and varied duties.

When winter weather results in cars sliding off township roads or the nearby interstate highway, drivers appreciate the prompt arrival of a police officer. Approximately 55 men and women who have chosen policing as their career are dedicated to protecting and serving township residents and are committed to earning the respect of the community by providing the highest standard of professionalism, integrity, and courage.

The arrival of McGruff the Crime Dog, accompanied by police officers and township officials, is a highlight for children attending a neighborhood block party during the annual National Night Out crime and drug prevention event in August. The township's celebration, which includes a kickoff at the Dayton Mall, as well as the block parties, was recognized as a national award winner by the National Association of Town Watch in 2002 and 2003.

Station No.3 firefighters and members of the station's ladies' auxiliary posed for this group picture in 1955. Fire Chief Schroeder (fifth from left) was joined by firefighters as follow, from left: P. Wasson, E. Akers, T. Yeazel, Captain G. Long, Lieutenant E. Hammond, V. Weber, L. Times, Lieutenant L. Toms, and C. Rice. Auxiliary members are, from left: Shirley Wasson, Esther Yeazel, Vera Long, Mrs. Hammond, Bea Weber, Annabelle Times, and Betty Toms.

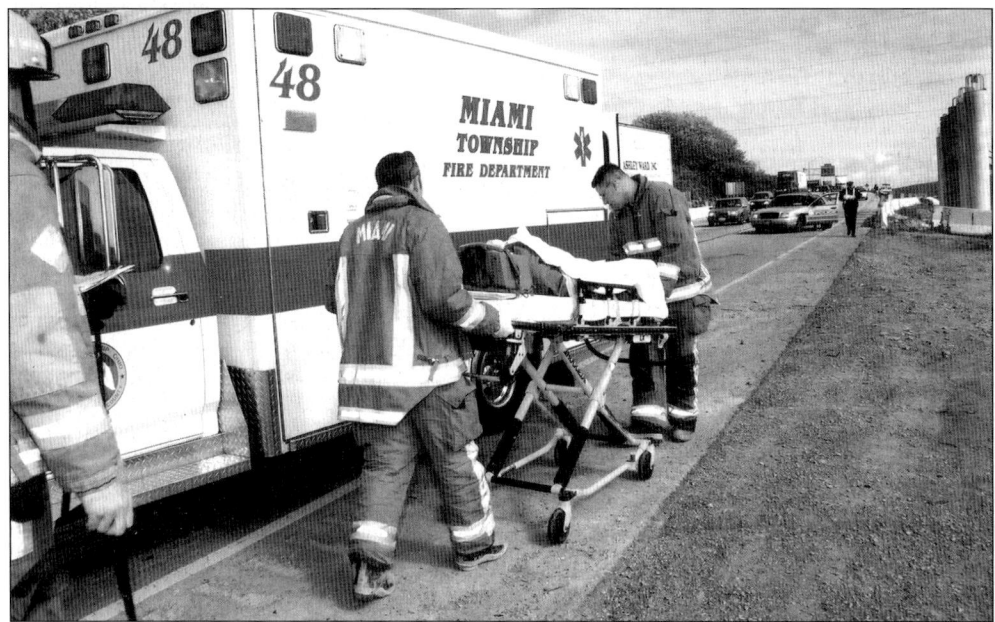

Today's Fire Department, made up of more than 70 men and women, provides a full range of protection, suppression, and emergency medical services from four stations located throughout the township. The equipment regularly deployed during emergencies, such as this accident on Lyons Road, includes three medic vehicles, six pumpers, one ladder truck, and one rescue vehicle.

Although the majority of the calls received by the department are for medical emergencies and fire-related incidents, occasionally there's a special call—and that's when members of the Special Operations group jump into action. They handle hazardous materials incidents and technical rescues, such as vehicle extrication, water rescue (pictured here), ice rescue, high-angle rope rescue, confined space rescue, trench rescue, and structural collapse.

Department members attend National Night Out block parties, sponsor fire station visits, offer CPR training, and visit township homes for fire detector testing and maintenance. In addition to increasing the firefighters' contact with the people they serve, these public education, planning, and inspection services help provide a high level of protection and low-cost insurance to township residents and businesses.

The oldest of Miami Township's departments was formed in the 1830s as the Road Department. This photograph, taken outside the township garage in 1937, pictures five men who provided a variety of services to the township and its residents. Today's Service Department still performs duties that are more diverse than any other department—but its mission is simple: to provide first-rate maintenance of township property. (Courtesy of the Mote family, Huston Beals photograph.)

The Service Department is made up of four units, each focusing on a defined area of responsibility. Members of the Parks Department oversee litter and weed control, tree pruning, and the general maintenance of eight township-operated parks. Their installation of "Kids Kube" playground equipment is much appreciated by the children who visit Layer, Miami View, Waldruhe, and Zengel Parks.

Road Department crews tend to the general maintenance of township roads and roadsides, from snow and leaf removal to street repair. This department also ensures that work performed on roads and rights-of-way by private contractors and property owners conform to township standards. The other two Service Department units, the Building Maintenance and Vehicle Maintenance departments, have responsibility for the buildings and vehicles used by the township's administration, police, fire, and service operations.

Members of the township's Parks and Recreation Board serve in a committee capacity to organize recreation-related events. For a number of years, they sponsored a December "Breakfast with Santa" for young children, held in the Chautauqua community center. Today, the Park Board sponsors a holiday decorating contest with prizes awarded to the residents whose homes exhibit the most attractive lighting displays.

Each spring, the Park Board sponsors an Easter egg hunt for children between the ages of one and ten. Held on the Saturday before Easter, the hunt takes place at Miami View Park. The Easter Bunny always visits the park to meet the children, and plenty of candy-filled plastic eggs are ready to be found. Most years, the bunny arrives on a township fire truck; sometimes there's another special visitor, like a clown who makes balloon figures. (Courtesy of Paul Tucker.)

A cane pole fishing derby is another spring event sponsored by the all-volunteer Park Board. Usually held in early May, while the weather is still cool enough for the fish to bite, the fishing derby takes place at Miami View Park, where the pond is specially stocked for the event. The Park Board provides extra poles, bait, and prizes or participation gifts. The anglers (between the ages of four and twelve) and their families also enjoy a free lunch. (Courtesy of Paul Tucker.)

Ghosts, goblins, and creatures of all descriptions roam the Waldruhe Park trail in October when the Park Board, assisted by the township's Service Department, hosts the annual Haunted Forest. Families walk along a half-mile path in the park where a number of scary creatures hide. More than 2,000 people usually visit the event and enjoy refreshments and a campfire (sometimes even a hayride) after their walk through the woods.

The Planning and Zoning Department is responsible for guiding land use and development, and the enforcement of zoning and property maintenance. The duties of its code enforcement officer include investigating and posting nuisance abatement notices (pictured above) and removing signs from township rights-of-way. The department's senior planner reviews land use issues and zoning (below) for new development and redevelopment, and approves site development plans. Working with the department are township volunteers who serve on the Board of Zoning Appeals and on the Zoning Commission.

Trash pickup service has been provided to township residents since the mid-1950s. Funded through a levy, the service includes weekly curbside pickup of trash and recyclables from all single-family homes and several apartment complexes. Bulk item pickup of water heaters, stoves, carpet rolls, tires, and other large items is also provided weekly by prior arrangement. (Courtesy of Paul Tucker.)

Once a month, the Combined Health District of Montgomery County's Immunization Clinic provides free childhood immunizations at the township's government center on Lyons Road. A registered nurse administers the shots to children of all ages. There are no family income requirements to receive immunizations, and the vaccines are of the highest quality. (Courtesy of Paul Tucker.)

The Miami Township Branch Library is located on Lyons Road just west of the township government center. The facility, which opened in August 2000, offers books, magazines, videotapes, CDs, cassettes, and DVD movies, as well as computer workstations with Internet access. During the library's dedication ceremony, the Community Foundation of Miami Township donated a check for $500—and a rocking chair for reading and relaxing. (Courtesy of Paul Tucker.)

Cox Arboretum and Gardens MetroPark on Springboro Pike in Miami Township is a living museum that includes 189 acres of natural wooded areas and specialty gardens, featuring plants suitable for the Miami Valley area. The arboretum offers numerous educational programs, three and a half miles of walking trails, ponds, bridges, a pavilion, park benches, and arbors, as well as unique birds and wildflowers. (Courtesy of Paul Tucker.)

Further Reading

Burke, Thomas Aquinas. *Ohio Lands: A Short History*. Columbus, Ohio: Auditor of State Jim Petro, 1997.

Everts, L.H. *Combination Atlas Map of Montgomery County, Ohio, 1875*. Evansville, Indiana: Unigraphic, Inc. reproduction, 1972.

Frush, Selma, editor. *Hometown Heritage: West Carrollton, Ohio, 1976*. West Carrollton, Ohio: West Carrollton Historical Society, 1976.

History of Montgomery County, Ohio, The. Chicago: W.H. Beers & Co., 1882. Evansville, Indiana: Unigraphic, Inc. reproduction, 1973.

Johnson, Mary Ann. *A Field Guide to Flight: On the Aviation Trail in Dayton, Ohio*; revised edition. Dayton, Ohio: Landfall Press, 1996.

Knepper, Dr. George W. *The Official Ohio Lands Book*. Columbus, Ohio: Auditor of State Jim Petro, 2002.

Light, Esther, and Mady Ransdell. *Miamisburg: The Story of Our Town*. Miamisburg, Ohio: Miamisburg Lions Club, 1993.

Miamisburg/West Carrollton News, The. 1900 to present.

"Mini-History of West Carrollton, A." West Carrollton, Ohio: The Ladies of the Research Club, n.d.

Moorehead, Warren King. *The Indian Tribes of Ohio* (reprinted from the Ohio Archeological and Historical Publications, Volume VII, 1899). Westerville, Ohio: Smoke & Fire Company, n.d.

O'Gorman, John. *Our Lady of Good Hope, Miamisburg, Ohio: Sesquicentennial History 1852–2002*. Dayton, Ohio: Meyers Printing & Design, Inc., 2002.

Puderbaugh, D.A., editor. *Montgomery County History and Annual*. Dayton, Ohio: Christian Publishing Association, 1926.

That Winter of '78. Dayton, Ohio: *Dayton Daily News* special edition, 1978.

Tibbals, Seymour. *Miami Valley Chautauqua: Then and Now*. Chautauqua, Ohio: Miami Valley Chautauqua Association, 1946.

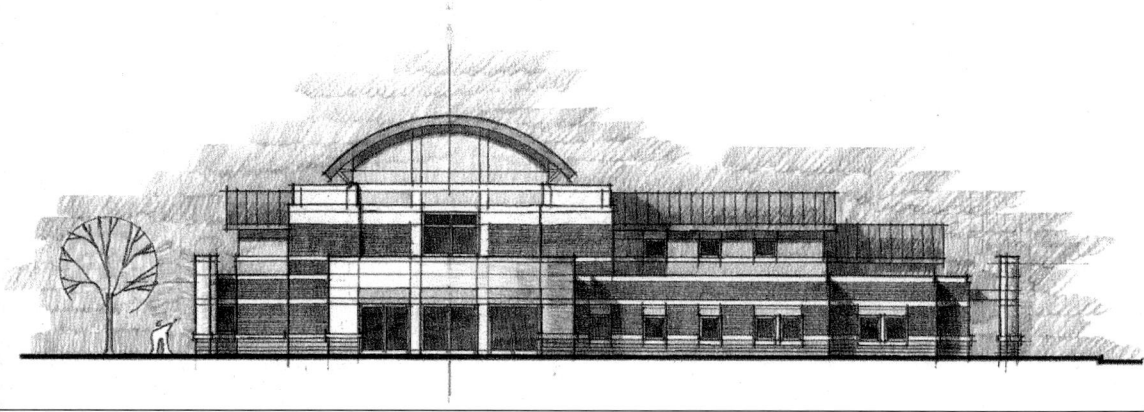

As Miami Township prepares to celebrate its 175th anniversary, plans were announced to build a $3.4 million full-service administration building on land south of the present government center on Lyons Road. The two-story building will include an emergency operations center, community room, trustees' meeting room, conference room, and offices. Groundbreaking for the new facility was scheduled to take place in August 2004.

An important feature of the new building is its standing or "dedicated" emergency operations center, which could be immediately activated in a crisis. This center will give the township greater flexibility in responding to emergencies and will provide backup for communications and power needs.

The building is seen as an investment in the future of the township—which is again undergoing a time of transition. When the new Austin Road interchange on Interstate 75 opens, Miami Township is certain to experience additional demands for services. Its elected officials, administrator, and staff are saying to the community, "We're going to be around for a long time, and we need to build something that looks to our future."

> "Time present and time past
> Are both perhaps present in time future,
> And time future contained in time past."
>
> —T.S. Eliot

Very little remains of Miami Township's "time past." Some farmland still exists, as do the white oak trees in Waldruhe Park. Once a rough footpath, the Mad River Road has been paved. Daniel Gebhart's tavern is now a museum.

"Time present" is the urban township, with its modern homes, condominiums, and apartment complexes, interstate highways, and the Dayton Mall. "Time future" is sure to be one of transition, of challenges, of new responsibilities.

Times change—but the Great Miami River remains, as does a township that places great value in its long tradition of service, its remaining green space, and the people and progress brought to it over the years by its "beautiful river." (Drawing from Cole and Russell Architects, Inc.)